1ˢᵗ World Library Literary Society

Giving Back to the World

"If you want to work on the core problem, it's early school literacy."

- James Barksdale, former CEO of Netscape

"No skill is more crucial to the future of a child, or to a democratic and prosperous society, than literacy."

- Los Angeles Times

"Literacy... means far more than learning how to read and write... The aim is to transmit... knowledge and promote social participation."

- UNESCO

"Literacy is not a luxury, it is a right and a responsibility. If our world is to meet the challenges of the twenty-first century we must harness the energy and creativity of all our citizens."

- President Bill Clinton

"Parents should be encouraged to read to their children, and teachers should be equipped with all available techniques for teaching literacy, so the varying needs and capacities of individual kids can be taken into account."

- Hugh Mackay

TOM SLADE MOTORCYCLE DISPATCH-BEARER

PERCY KEESE FITZHUGH

1st WORLD
LIBRARY
Literary Society

Tom Slade Motorcycle Dispatch Bearer

Percy Keese Fitzhugh

© 1st World Library, 2009
PO Box 2211
Fairfield, IA 52556
www.1stworldlibrary.com
First Edition

LCCN: 2009923484

Softcover ISBN: 978-1-4218-8872-9
Hardcover ISBN: 978-1-4218-8971-9
eBook ISBN: 978-1-4218-8773-9

Purchase *"Tom Slade Motorcycle Dispatch Bearer"*
as a traditional bound book at:
www.1stWorldLibrary.com/purchase.asp?ISBN=978-1-4218-8872-9

1st World Library is a literary, educational organization
dedicated to:

- Creating a free internet library of downloadable ebooks

- Hosting writing competitions and offering book publishing
scholarships.

Interested in more 1st World Library books? contact:
literacy@1stworldlibrary.com
Check us out at: www.1stworldlibrary.com

CONTENTS

PREFACE

It was good advice that Rudyard Kipling gave his "young British soldier" in regard to the latter's rifle:

"She's human as you are—you treat her as sich
And she'll fight for the young British soldier."

Tommy Atkins' rifle was by no means the first inanimate or dumb thing to prove human and to deserve human treatment. Animals of all sorts have been given this quality. Jack London's dog, in *The Call of the Wild*, has human interest. So has the immortal *Black Beauty*.

But we are not concerned with animals now. Kipling's ocean liner has human interest—a soul. I need not tell you that a boat is human. Its every erratic quality of crankiness, its veritable heroism under stress, its temperament (if you like that word) makes it very human indeed. That is why a man will often let his boat rot rather than sell it.

This is not true of all inanimate things. It depends. I have never heard of a steam roller or a poison gas bomb being beloved by anybody. I should not care to associate with a hand grenade. It is a matter of taste; I dare say I could learn to love a British tank, but I could never make a friend and confidante of a balloon. An aeroplane might prove a good pal—we shall have to see.

Davy Crockett actually made a friend and confidante of his famous gun, *Betsy*. And *Betsy* is known in history. It is said that the gun crews on armed liners have found this human quality in their guns, and many of these have been given names—*Billy Sunday*, *Teddy Roosevelt*, etc.

I need not tell you that a camp-fire is human and that trees are human.

The pioneers of old, pressing into the dim wilderness, christened their old flintlocks and talked to them as a man may talk to a man. The woodsman's axe was "deare and greatly beloved," we are told.

The hard-pressed Indian warrior knelt in the forest and besought that life-long comrade, his bow, not to desert or fail him. King Philip kept in his quiver a favorite arrow which he never used because it had earned retirement by saving his own life.

What Paul Revere may have said to his horse in that stirring midnight ride we do not know. But may we not suppose that he urged his trusty steed forward with resolute and inspiring words about the glorious errand they were upon?

Perhaps the lonely ringer of the immortal bell up in the Old South steeple muttered some urgent word of incentive to that iron clanger as it beat against its ringing wall of brass.

So I have made *Uncle Sam*, the motorcycle, the friend and companion of *Tom Slade*. I have withheld none of their confidences—or trifling differences. I dare say they were both weary and impatient at times.

Percy Keese Fitzhugh

If he is not companionable to you, then so much the worse for you and for our story. But he was the friend, the inseparable associate and co-patriot of *Tom Slade, the Dispatch Rider.*

You will not like him any the less because of the noise he made in trudging up a hill, or because his mud-guard was broken off, or his tire wounded in the great cause, or his polished headlight knocked into a tin can. You will not ridicule the old splint of a shingle which was bound with such surgical nicety among his rusting spokes. If you do, then you are the kind of a boy who would laugh at a wounded soldier and you had better not read this book.

CHAPTER ONE

FOR SERVICE AS REQUIRED

Swiftly and silently along the moonlit road sped the dispatch-rider. Out of the East he had come, where the battle line runs between blue mountains and the country is quiet and peaceful, and the boys in khaki long for action and think wistfully of Picardy and Flanders. He was a lucky young fellow, this dispatch-rider, and all the boys had told him so.

"We'll miss you, Thatchy," they had said.

And "Thatchy" had answered characteristically, "I'm sorry, too, kind of, in a way."

His name was not Thatchy, but they had called him so because his thick shock of light hair, which persisted in falling down over his forehead and ears, had not a little the appearance of the thatched roofs on the French peasant's cottages. He, with a loquacious young companion, had blown into the Toul sector from no one seemed to know exactly where, more than that he had originally been a ship's boy, had been in a German prison camp, and had escaped through Alsace and reached the American forces after a perilous journey.

Percy Keese Fitzhugh

Lately he had been running back and forth on his motorcycle between the lines and points south in a region which had not been defiled by the invader, but now he was going far into the West "for service as required."

That was what the slip of paper from headquarters had said, and he did not speculate as to what those services would be, but he knew that they would not be exactly holding Sunday-School picnics in the neighborhood of Montdidier. Billy Brownway, machine gunner, had assured Thatchy that undoubtedly he was wanted to represent the messenger service on the War Council at Versailles. But Thatchy did not mind that kind of talk.

West of Revigny, he crossed the old trench line, and came into the area which the Blond Beast had crossed and devastated in the first year of the war. Planks lay across the empty trenches and as he rode over first the French and then the enemy ditches, he looked down and could see in the moonlight some of the ghastly trophies of war. Somehow they affected him more than had the fresher results of combat which he had seen even in the quiet sector he had left.

Silently he sped along the thirty-mile stretch from Revigny to Chalons, where a little group of French children pressed about him when he paused for gasoline.

"Yankee!" they called, chattering at him and meddling with his machine.

"Le cheveu!" one brazen youngster shouted, running his hand through his own hair by way of demonstrating Thatchy's most conspicuous characteristic.

Thatchy poked him good-humoredly. "La route, est-belle

bonne?" he asked.

The child nodded enthusiastically, while the others broke out laughing at Thatchy's queer French, and poured a verbal torrent at him by way of explaining that the road to the South would take him through Vertus and Montmirail, while the one to the north led to Epernay.

"I'll bump my nose into the salient if I take that one," he said more to himself than to them, but one little fellow, catching the word *salient* took a chance on *nose* and jumped up and down in joyous abandon, calling, "Bump le nez—le *salient!*" apparently in keen appreciation of the absurdity of the rider's phrase.

He rode away with a clamoring chorus behind him and he heard one brazen youngster boldly mimicking his manner of asking if the roads were good. These children lived in tumble-down houses which were all but ruins, and played in shell holes as if these cruel, ragged gaps in the earth had been made by the kind Boche for their especial entertainment.

A mile or two west of Chalons the rider crossed the historic Marne on a makeshift bridge built from the materials of a ruined house and the remnants of the former span.

On he sped, along the quiet, moonlit road, through the little village of Thibie, past many a quaint old heavily-roofed brick cottage, over the stream at Chaintrix and into Vertus, and along the straight, even stretch of road for Montmirail. Not so long ago he might have gone from Chalons in a bee-line from Montdidier, but the big, ugly salient stuck out like a huge snout now, as if it were sniffing in longing antici-pation at that tempting morsel, Paris; so he must circle around it and then turn almost straight north.

At La Ferte, among the hills, he paused at a crossroads and, alighting from his machine, stood watching as a long, silent procession of wagons passed by in the quiet night, moving southward. He knew now what it meant to go into the West. One after another they passed in deathlike stillness, the Red Cross upon the side of each plainly visible in the moonlight. As he paused, the rider could hear the thunder of great guns in the north. Many stretchers, borne by men afoot, followed the wagons and he could hear the groans of those who tossed restlessly upon them.

"Look out for shell holes," he heard someone say. So there were Americans in the fighting, he thought.

He ran along the edge of the hills now on the fifteen-mile stretch to Meaux, where he intended to follow the road northward through Senlis and across the old trenches near Clermont. He could hear the booming all the while, but it seemed weary and spent, like a runner who has slackened his pace and begun to pant.

At Meaux he crossed the path of another silent cavalcade of stretchers and ambulances and wounded soldiers who were being supported as they limped along. They spoke in French and one voice came out of an ambulance, seeming hollow and far off, as though from a grave. Then came a lot of German prisoners tramping along, some sullen and some with a fine air of bravado sneering at their guards.

The rider knew where he was going and how to get there and he did not venture any inquiries either as to his way or what had been going on.

Happenings in Flanders and Picardy are known in America before they are known to the boys in Alsace. He knew there was fighting in the West and that Fritz had poked a big bulge into the French line, for his superiors had given him a road map with the bulge pencilled upon it so that he might go around it and not bump his nose into it, as he had said. But he had not expected to see such obvious signs of fighting and it made him realize that at last he was getting into the war with a vengeance.

Instead of following the road leading northwest out of Meaux, he took the one leading northeast up through Villers-Cotterets, intending to run along the edge of the forest to Campiegne and then verge westward to the billet villages northwest of Montdidier, where he was to report.

This route brought him within ten miles of the west arm of the salient, but the way was quiet and there was no sign of the fighting as he rode along in the woody solitude. It reminded him of his home far back in America and of the woods where he and his scout companions had camped and hiked and followed the peaceful pursuits of stalking and trailing.

He was thinking of home as he rode leisurely along the winding forest road, when suddenly he was startled by a rustling sound among the trees.

"Who goes there?" he demanded in pursuance of his general instructions for such an emergency, at the same time drawing his pistol. "Halt!"

He was the scout again now, keen, observant. But there was no answer to his challenge and he narrowed his eyes to mere slits, peering into the tree-studded solitude, waiting.

Then suddenly, close by him he heard that unmistakable sound, the clanking of a chain, and accompanying it a voice saying, "Kamerad."

Percy Keese Fitzhugh

CHAPTER TWO

AID AND COMFORT TO THE ENEMY

Tom Slade, dispatch-rider, knew well enough what *kamerad* meant. He had learned at least that much of German warfare and German honor, even in the quiet Toul sector. He knew that the German olive branch was poisoned; that German treachery was a fine art—a part of the German efficiency. Had not Private Coleburn, whom Tom knew well, listened to that kindly uttered word and been stabbed with a Prussian bayonet in the darkness of No Man's Land?

"Stand up," said Tom. "Nobody can talk to *me* crouching down like that."

"Ach!" said the voice in the unmistakable tone of pain. "Vot goot—see!"

Tom turned on his searchlight and saw crawling toward him a German soldier, hatless and coatless, whose white face seemed all the more pale and ghastly for the smear of blood upon it. He was quite without arms, in proof of which he raised his open hands and slapped his sides and hips. As he did so a long piece of heavy chain, which was manacled to his wrist clanged and rattled.

"Ach!" he said, shaking his head as if in agony.

"Put your hands down. All right," said Tom. "Can you speak English?"

"Kamerad," he repeated and shrugged his shoulders as if that were enough.

"You escape?" said Tom, trying to make himself understood. "How did you get back of the French lines?"

"Shot broke—yach," the man said, his face lapsing again into a hopeless expression of suffering.

"All right," said Tom, simply. "Comrade—I say it too. All right?"

The soldier's face showed unmistakable relief through his suffering.

"Let's see what's the matter," Tom said, though he knew the other only vaguely understood him. Turning the wheel so as the better to focus the light upon the man, he saw that he had been wounded in the foot, which was shoeless and bleeding freely, but that the chief cause of his suffering was the raw condition of his wrist where the manacle encircled it and the heavy chain pulled. It seemed to Tom as if this cruel sore might have been caused by the chain dragging behind him and perhaps catching on the ground as he fled.

"The French didn't put that on?" he queried, rather puzzled.

The soldier shook his head. "Herr General," said he.

"Not the Americans?"

"Herr General—gun."

Then suddenly there flashed into Tom's mind something he had heard about German artillerymen being chained to their guns. So that was it. And some French gunner, or an American maybe, had unconsciously set this poor wretch free by smashing his chain with a shell.

"You're in the French lines," Tom said. "Did you mean to come here? You're a prisoner."

"Ach, diss iss petter," the man said, only half understanding.

"Yes, I guess it is," said Tom. "I'll bind your foot up and then I'll take that chain off if I can and bind your wrist. Then we'll have to find the nearest dressing station. I suppose you got lost in this forest. I been in the German forest myself," he added; "it's fine—better than this. I got to admit they've got fine lakes there."

Whether he said this by way of comforting the stranger— though he knew the man understood but little of it—or just out of the blunt honesty which refused to twist everything German into a thing of evil, it would be hard to say. He had about him that quality of candor which could not be shaken even by righteous enmity.

Tearing two strips from his shirt, he used the narrower one to make a tourniquet, which he tied above the man's ankle.

"If you haven't got poison in it, it won't be so bad," he said. "Now I'll take off that chain."

He raised his machine upon its rest so that the power wheel was free of the ground. Then, to the wounded Boche's puzzled surprise, he removed the tire and fumbling in his little tool kit he took out a piece of emery cloth which he used for cleaning his plugs and platinum contact points, and bent it over the edge of the rim, binding it to the spokes with the length of insulated wire which he always carried. It was a crude and makeshift contrivance at best, but at last he succeeded, by dint of much bending and winding and tying of the pliable copper wire among the spokes of the wheel, in fastening the emery cloth over the fairly sharp rim so that it stayed in place when he started his power and in about two revolutions it cut a piece of wire with which he tested the power of his improvised mechanical file.

"Often I sharpened a jackknife that way on the fly-wheel of a motor boat," he said. The Boche did not understand him, but he was quick to see the possibilities of this whirling hacksaw and he seemed to acknowledge, with as much grace as a German may, the Yankee ingenuity of his liberator.

"Give me your wrist," said Tom, reaching for it; "I won't hurt it any more than I have to; here—here's a good scheme."

He carefully stuffed his handkerchief around under the metal band which encircled the soldier's wrist and having thus formed a cushion to receive the pressure and protect the raw flesh, he closed his switch again and gently subjected the manacle to the revolving wheel, holding it upon the edge of the concave tire bed.

If the emery cloth had extended all the way around the wheel he could have taken the manacle off in less time than it had taken Kaiser Bill to lock it on, for the contrivance rivalled a buzzsaw. As it was, he had to stop every minute or two to rearrange the worn emery cloth and bind it in place anew. But for all that he succeeded in less than fifteen minutes in working a furrow almost through the metal band so that a little careful manipulating and squeezing and pressing of it

Percy Keese Fitzhugh

enabled him to break it and force it open.

"There you are," he said, removing the handkerchief so as to get a better look at the cruel sore beneath; "didn't hurt much, did it? That's what Uncle Sam's trying to do for all the rest of you fellers—only you haven't got sense enough to know it."

CHAPTER THREE

THE OLD COMPASS

Tom took the limping Boche, his first war prisoner, to the Red Cross station at Vivieres where they had knives and scissors and bandages and antiseptics, but nothing with which to remove Prussian manacles, and all the king's horses and all the king's men and the willing, kindly nurses there could have done little for the poor Boche if Tom Slade, alias Thatchy, had not administered his own particular kind of first aid.

The French doctors sent him forth with unstinted praise which he only half understood, and as he sped along the road for Compiegne he wondered who could have been the allied gunner who at long range had cut Fritzie loose from the piece of artillery to which he had been chained.

"That feller and I did a good job anyway," he thought.

At Compiegne the whole town was in a ferment as he passed through. Hundreds of refugees with mule carts and wheelbarrows laden with their household goods, were leaving the town in anticipation of the German advance. They made a mournful procession as they passed out of the town along the south road with babies crying and children clamoring about

Percy Keese Fitzhugh

the clumsy, overladen vehicles. He saw many boys in khaki here and there and it cheered and in-spired him to know that his country was represented in the fighting. He had to pause in the street to let a company of them pass by on their way northward to the trench line and it did his heart good to hear their cheery laughter and typical American banter.

"Got any cigarettes, kiddo?" one called.

"Where you going—north?" asked another.

"To the billets west of Montdidier," Tom answered. "I'm for new service. I came from Toul sector."

"Good-*night*! That's Sleepy Hollow over there."

From Compiegne he followed the road across the Aronde and up through Mery and Tricot into Le Cardonnois. The roads were full of Americans and as he passed a little company of them he called,

"How far is—?" naming the village of his destination.

"About two miles," one of them answered; "straight north."

"Tell 'em to give 'em Hell," another called.

This laconic utterance was the first intimation which Tom had that anything special was brewing in the neighborhood, and he answered with characteristic literalness, "All right, I will."

The road northward from Le Cardonnois was through a hilly country, where there were few houses. About half a mile farther on he reached the junction of another road which appeared also to lead northward, verging slightly in an easterly direction. He had made so many turns that he was a little puzzled as to which was the true north road, so he stopped and took out the trusty little compass which he always carried, and held it in the glare of his headlight, thinking to verify his course. Undoubtedly the westward road was the one leading to his destination for as he walked a little way along the other road he found that it bent still more to the eastward and he believed that it must reach the French front after another mile or two.

As he looked again at the cheap, tin-encased compass he smiled a little ruefully, for it reminded him of Archibald Archer, with whom he had escaped from the prison camp in Germany and made his perilous flight through the Black Forest into Switzerland and to the American forces near Toul.

Archibald Archer! Where, in all that war-scourged country, was Archibald Archer now, Tom wondered. No doubt, chatting familiarly with generals and field marshals somewhere, in blithe disregard of dignity and authority; for he was a brazen youngster and an indefatigable souvenir hunter.

So vivid were Tom's thoughts of Archer that, being off his machine, he sat down by the roadside to eat the rations which his anxiety to reach his destination had deterred him from eating before.

"That's just like him," he thought, holding the compass out so that it caught the subdued rays of his dimmed headlight; "always marking things up, or whittling his initials or looking for souvenirs."

The particular specimen of Archer's handiwork which opened this train of reminiscence was part and parcel of the mischievous habit which apparently had begun very early in his career, when he renovated the habiliments of the heroes and statesmen in his school geography by pencilling high hats and sunbonnets on their honored heads and giving them flowing moustaches and frock coats.

In the prison camp from which they had escaped he had carved his initials on fence and shack, but his masterpiece was the conversion of the N on this same glassless compass into a very presentable S (though turned sideways) and the S into a very presentable N.

The occasion of his doing this was a singular experience the two boys had had in their flight through Germany when, after being carried across a lake on a floating island while asleep, they had swum back and retraced their steps northward supposing that they were still going south.

"Either we're wrong or the compass is wrong, Slady," the bewildered Archer had said, and he had forthwith altered the compass points before they discovered the explanation of their singular experience.

After reaching the American forces Archer had gone forth to more adventures and new glories in the transportation department, the line of his activities being between Paris and the coast, and Tom had seen him no more. He had given the compass to Tom as a "souvenir," and Tom, whose sober nature had found much entertainment in Archer's sprightliness, had cherished it as such. It was useful sometimes, too, though he had to be careful always to remember that it was the "wrong way round."

"He'll turn up like a bad penny some day," he thought now, smiling a little. "He said he'd bring me the clock from a Paris cathedral for a souvenir, and he'd change the twelve to twenty-two on it."

He remembered that he had asked Archer *what* cathedral in Paris, and Archer had answered, "The Cathedral de la Plaster of Paris."

"He's a sketch," thought Tom.

CHAPTER FOUR

THE OLD FAMILIAR FACES

"That's the way it is," thought Tom, "you get to know fellers and like 'em, and then you get separated and you don't see 'em any more."

Perhaps he was the least bit homesick, coming into this new sector where all were strangers to him. In any event, as he sat there finishing his meal he fell to thinking of the past and of the "fellers" he had known. He had known a good many for despite his soberness there was something about him which people liked. Most of his friends had taken delight in jollying him and he was one of those boys who are always being nicknamed wherever they go. Over in the Toul sector they "joshed" and "kidded" him from morning till night but woe be to you if you had sought to harm him!

He had been sorry, in a way, to leave the Toul sector, just as he had been sorry to leave Bridgeboro when he got his first job on a ship. "That's one thing fellers can't understand," he thought, "how you can be sorry about a thing and glad too. Girls understand better—I'll say that much for 'em, even though I—even though they never had much use for me—"

He fell to thinking of the scout troop of which he had been a member away back in America, of Mr. Ellsworth, the scout-master, who had lifted him out of the gutter, and of Roy Blakeley who was always fooling, and Peewee Harris. Peewee must be quite a boy by now—not a tenderfootlet any more, as Roy had called him.

And then there was Rossie Bent who worked in the bank and who had run away the night before Registration Day, hoping to escape military service. Tom fell to thinking of him and of how he had traced him up to a lonely mountain top and made him go back and register just in time to escape disgrace and punishment.

"He thought he was a coward till he got the uniform on," he thought. "That's what makes the difference. I bet he's one of the bravest soldiers over here now. Funny if I should meet him. I always liked him anyway, even when people said he was conceited. Maybe he had a right to be. If girls liked me as much as they did him maybe *I'd* be conceited. Anyway, I'd like to see him again, that's one sure thing."

When he had finished his meal he felt of his tires, gave his grease cup a turn, mounted his machine and was off to the north for whatever awaited him there, whether it be death or glory or just hard work; and to new friends whom he would meet and part with, who doubtless would "josh" him and make fun of his hair and tell him extravagant yarns and belittle and discredit his soberly and simply told "adventures," and yet who would like him nevertheless.

"That's the funny thing about some fellers," he thought, "you never can tell whether they like you or not. Rossie used to say girls were hard to understand, but, gee, I think fellers are harder!"

Swiftly and silently along the moonlit road he sped, the

dispatch-rider who had come from the blue hills of Alsace across the war-scorched area into the din and fire and stenching suffocation and red-running streams of Picardy "for service as required." Two miles behind the straining line he rode and parallel with it, straight northward, keeping his keen, steady eyes fixed upon the road for shell holes. Over to the east he could hear the thundering boom of artillery and once the air just above him seemed to buzz as if some mammoth wasp had passed. But he rode steadily, easily, without a tremor.

When he dismounted in front of headquarters at the little village of his destination his stolid face was grimy from his long ride and the dust of the blue Alsatian mountains mingled with the dust of devastated France upon his khaki uniform (which was proper and fitting) and his rebellious hair was streaky and matted and sprawled down over his frowning forehead.

A little group of soldiers gathered about him after he had given his paper to the commanding officer, for he had come a long way and they knew the nature of his present service if he did not. They watched him rather curiously, for it was not customary to bring a dispatch-rider from such a distance when there were others available in the neighborhood. He was the second sensation of that memorable night, for scarcely two hours before General Pershing himself had arrived and he was at that very minute in conference with other officers in the little red brick cottage. Even as the group of soldiers clustered about the rider, officers hurried in and out with maps, and one young fellow, an aviator apparently, suddenly emerged and hurried away.

"What's going to be doing?" Tom asked, taking notice of all these activities and speaking in his dull way.

Evidently the boys had already taken his measure and formulated their policy, for one answered,

"Peace has been declared and they're trying to decide whether we'd better take Berlin or have it sent C.O.D."

"A soldier I met a couple of miles back," said Tom, "told me to tell you to give 'em Hell."

It was characteristic of him that although he never used profanity he delivered the soldier's message exactly as it had been given him.

CHAPTER FIVE

GETTING READY

Tom wheeled his machine over to a long brick cottage which stood flush with the road and attended to it with the same care and affection as a man might show a favorite horse. Then he sat down with several others on a long stone bench and waited.

There was something in the very air which told him that important matters were impending and though he believed that they had not expected him to arrive just at this time he wondered whether he might not be utilized now that he was here. So he sat quietly where he was, observant of everything, but asking no questions.

There was a continuous stream of officers entering and emerging from the headquarters opposite and twice within half an hour companies of soldiers were brought into formation and passed silently away along the dark road.

"You'll be in Germany in a couple of hours," called a private sitting alongside Tom as some of them passed.

"Cantigny isn't Germany," another said.

"Sure it is," retorted a third; "all the land they hold is German soil. Call us up when you get a chance," he added in a louder tone to the receding ranks.

"Is Cantigny near here?" Tom asked.

"Just across the ditches."

"Are we going to try to take it?"

"*Try* to? We're going to wrap it up and bring it home."

Tom was going to ask the soldier if he thought there would be any chance for *him*, though he knew well enough that his business was behind the lines and that the most he could hope for was to carry the good news (if such it proved to be) still farther back, away from the fighting.

"This is going to be the first offensive of your old Uncle Samuel and if we don't get the whole front page in the New York papers we'll be peeved," Tom's neighbor condescended to inform him.

Whatever Uncle Samuel was up to he was certainly very busy about it and very quiet. On the little village green which the cottage faced groups of officers talked earnestly.

An enormous spool on wheels, which in the darkness seemed a mile high, was rolled silently from somewhere or other, the wheels staked and bound to the ground, and braces were erected against it. Very little sound was made and there were no lights save in the houses, which all to be swarming with soldiers. Not a civilian was to be seen. Several soldiers walked away from the big wheel and it moved around slowly like one of those gigantic passenger-carrying wheels in an amusement resort.

Percy Keese Fitzhugh

Presently some one remarked that Collie was in and there was a hurrying away—toward the rear of the village, as it seemed to Tom.

"Who's Collie?" he ventured to ask.

"Collie? Oh, he's the Stormy Petrel; he's been piking around over the Fritzies' heads, I s'pose."

Evidently Collie, or the Stormy Petrel, was an aviator who had alighted somewhere about the village with some sort of a report.

"Collie can't see in the daylight," his neighbor added; "he and the Jersey Snipe have got Fritzie vexed. You going to run between here and the coast?"

"I don't know what I'm going to do," said Tom. "I don't suppose I'll go over the top, I'd like to go to Cantigny."

"Never mind, they'll bring it back to you. Did you know the old gent is here?"

"Pershing?"

"Yup. Going to run the show himself."

"Are you going?"

"Not as far as I know. I was in the orchestra—front row— last week. Got a touch of trench fever."

"D'you mean the front line trenches?" Tom asked.

"Yup. Oh, look at Bricky!" he added suddenly. "You carrying wire, Bricky? There's a target for a sniper for you—hair as red as—"

"Just stick around at the other end of it," interrupted "Bricky" as he passed, "and listen to what you hear."

"Here come the tanks," said Tom's neighbor, "and there's the Jersey Snipe perched on the one over at the other end. Good-*night*, Fritzie!"

The whole scene reminded Tom vaguely of the hasty, quiet picking up and departure of the circus in the night which, as a little boy, he had sat up to watch. There were the tanks, half a dozen of them (and he knew there were more elsewhere), covered with soldiers and waiting in the darkness like elephants. Troops were constantly departing, for the front trenches he supposed.

Though he had never yet been before the lines, his experience as a rider and his close touch with the fighting men had given him a pretty good military sense in the matter of geography—that is, he understood now without being told the geographical relation of one place to another in the immediate neighborhood. Dispatch-riders acquire this sort of extra sense very quickly and they come to have a knowledge of the lay of the land infinitely more accurate than that of the average private soldier.

Tom knew that this village, which was now the scene of hurried preparation and mysterious comings and goings, was directly behind the trench area. He knew that somewhere back of the village was the artillery, and he believed that the village of Cantigny stood in the same relation to the German trenches that this billet village stood to the Allied trenches; that is, that it was just behind the German lines and that the German artillery was still farther back. He had heard enough talk about trench warfare to know how the Americans

Percy Keese Fitzhugh

intended to conduct this operation.

But he had never seen an offensive in preparation, either large or small, for there had been no American offensives— only raids, and of course he had not participated in these. It seemed to him that now, at last, he was drawn to the very threshold of active warfare only to be compelled to sit silent and gaze upon a scene every detail of which aroused his longing for action. The hurried consultation of officers, the rapid falling in line in the darkness, the clear brisk words of command, the quick mechanical response, the departure of one group after another, the thought of that aviator alighting behind the village, the sight of the great, ugly tanks and the big spool aroused his patriotism and his craving for adventure as nothing else had in all the months of his service. He was nearer to the trenches than ever before.

"If you're riding to Clermont," he heard a soldier say, apparently to him, "you'd better take the south road; turn out when you get to Airian. The other's full of shell holes from the old trench line."

"Best way is to go down through Estrees and follow the road back across the old trench line," said another.

Tom listened absently. He knew he could find the best way, that was his business, but he did not want to go to Clermont. It seemed to him that he was always going away from the war while others were going toward it. While these boys were rushing forward he would be rushing backward. That was always the way.

"There's a lot of skeletons in those old trenches. You can follow the ditches almost down to Paris."

"They won't send him farther than Creil," another said. "The wires are up all the way from Creil down."

"You never can tell whether they'll stay up or not—not with this seventy-five mile bean-shooter Fritzie's playing with. Ever been to Paris, kid?"

"No, but I s'pose I'll be sent there now—maybe," Tom answered.

"They'll keep you moving up this way, all right. You were picked for this sector—d'you know that?"

"I don't know why."

"Don't get rattled easy—that's what I heard."

This was gratifying if it was true. Tom had not known why he had been sent so far and he had wondered.

Presently a Signal Corps captain came out of Headquarters, spoke briefly with two officers who were near the big wire spool, and then turned toward the bench on which Tom was sitting. His neighbors arose and saluted and he did the same.

"Never been under fire, I suppose?" said the captain, addressing Tom to his great surprise.

"Not before the lines, I haven't. The machine I had before this one was knocked all out of shape by a shell. I was riding from Toul to—"

"All right," interrupted the captain somewhat impatiently. Tom was used to being interrupted in the midst of his sometimes rambling answers. He could never learn the good military rule of being brief and explicit. "How do you feel about going over the top? You don't have to."

"It's just what I was thinking about," said Tom eagerly. "If you'd be willing, I'd like to."

"Of course you'd be under fire. Care to volunteer? Emergency work."

"Often I wished—"

"Care to volunteer?"

"Yes, sir, I do."

"All right; go inside and get some sleep. They'll wake you up in about an hour. Machine in good shape?"

This was nothing less than an insult. "I always keep it in good shape," said Tom. "I got extra—"

"All right. Go in and get some sleep; you haven't got long. The wire boys will take care of you."

He strode away and began to talk hurriedly with another man who showed him some papers and Tom watched him as one in a trance.

"Now you're in for it, kiddo," he heard some one say.

"R. I. P. for yours," volunteered another.

Tom knew well enough what R. I. P. meant. Often in his lonely night rides through the towns close to the fighting he had seen it on row after row of rough, carved wooden crosses.

"There won't be much *resting in peace* to-night. How about it, Toul sector?"

"I didn't feel very sleepy, anyway," said Tom.

He slept upon one of the makeshift straw bunks on the stone floor of the cellar under the cottage. With the first streak of dawn he arose and went quietly out and sat on a powder keg under a small window, tore several pages out of his pocket blank-book and using his knee for a desk, wrote:

"DEAR MARGARET:

"Maybe you'll be surprised, kind of, to get a letter from me. And maybe you won't like me calling you Margaret. I told Roy to show you my letters, cause I knew he'd be going into Temple Camp office on account of the troop getting ready to go to Camp and I knew he'd see you. I'd like to be going up to camp with them, and I'd kind of like to be back in the office, too. I remember how I used to be scared of you and you said you must be worse than the Germans 'cause I wasn't afraid of them. I hope you're working there yet and I'd like to see Mr. Burton, too.

"I was going to write to Roy but I decided I'd send a letter to you because whenever something is going to happen the fellows write letters home and leave them to be mailed in case they don't get back. So if you get this you'll know I'm killed. Most of them write to girls or their mothers, and as long as I haven't got any mother I thought I'd write to you. Because maybe you'd like to hear I'm killed more than anybody. I mean maybe you'd be more interested.

"I'm going to go over the top with this regiment. I got sent way over to this sector for special service. A fellow told me he heard it was because I got a level head. I can't tell you where I am, but this morning we're going to take a town. I didn't have to go, 'cause I'm a non-com., but I volunteered. I don't know what I'll have to do.

"I ain't exactly scared, but it kind of makes me think about home and all like that. I often wished I'd meet Roscoe Bent over here. Maybe he wrote to you. I bet everybody likes him wherever he is over here. It's funny how I got to thinking about you last night. I'll—there goes the bugle, so I can't write any more. Anyway, you won't get it unless I'm killed. Maybe you won't like my writing, but every fellow writes to a girl the last thing. It seems kind of lonely if you can't write to a girl.

"Your friend,

"TOM SLADE."

CHAPTER SIX

OVER THE TOP

The first haze of dawn was not dispelled when the artillery began to thunder and Tom knew that the big job was on. Stolid as he was and used to the roar of the great guns, he made hasty work of his breakfast for he was nervous and anxious to be on the move.

Most of the troops that were to go seemed to have gone already. He joined the two signal corps men, one of whom carried the wire and the other a telephone apparatus, and as they moved along the road other signal corps men picked up the wire behind them at intervals, carrying it along.

Tom was as proud of his machine as a general could be of his horse, and he wheeled it along beside him, keeping pace with the slow advance of his companions, his heart beating high.

"If you have to come back with any message, you'll remember Headquarters, won't you?" one asked him.

"I always remember Headquarters," said Tom.

"And don't get rattled."

"I never get rattled."

"Watch the roads carefully as we go, so you can get back all right. Noise don't bother you?"

"No, I'm used to artillery—I mean the noise," said Tom.

"You probably won't have much to do unless in an emergency. If Fritzie cuts the wire or it should get tangled and we couldn't reach the airmen quick enough you'd have to beat it back. There's two roads out of Cantigny. Remember to take the south one. We're attacking on a mile front. If you took—"

"If I have to come back," said Tom, "I'll come the same way. You needn't worry."

His advisor felt sufficiently squelched. And indeed, he had no cause to worry. The Powers that Be had sent Thatchy into the West where the battle line was changing every day and roads were being made and destroyed and given new directions; where the highway which took one to Headquarters one day led into the lair of the Hun on the next, and all the land was topsy-turvy and changing like the designs in a kaleidoscope—for the very good reason that Thatchy invariably reached his destination and could be depended upon to come back, through all the chaos, as a cat returns to her home. The prison camps in Germany were not without Allied dispatch-riders who had become "rattled" and had blundered into the enemy's arms, but Thatchy had a kind of uncanny extra sense, a bump of locality, if you will, and that is why they had sent him into this geographical tangle where maps became out of date as fast as they were made.

The sun was not yet up when they reached a wider road running crossways to the one out of the village and here many troops were waiting as far up and down the road as

Tom could see. A narrow ditch led away from the opposite side of the road through the fields beyond, and looking up and down the road he could see that there were other ditches like it.

The tanks were already lumbering and waddling across the fields, for all the world like great clumsy mud turtles, with soldiers perched upon them as if they were having a straw ride. Before Tom and his companions entered the nearest ditch he could see crowds of soldiers disappearing into other ditches far up the road.

The fields above them were covered with shell holes, a little cemetery flanked one side of the zigzag way, and the big dugouts of the reserves were everywhere in this backyard of the trench area. Out of narrow, crooked side avenues soldiers poured into the communication trench which the wire carriers were following, falling in ahead of them.

"We'll get into the road after the boys go over and then you'll have more room for your machine. Close quarters, hey?" Tom's nearest companion said.

When they reached the second-line trench the boys were leaving it, by hundreds as it seemed to Tom, and crowding through the crooked communication trenches. The wire carriers followed on, holding up the wire at intervals. Once when Tom peeped over the edge of the communication trench he saw the tanks waddling along to right and left, rearing up and bowing as they crossed the trench, like clumsy, trained hippopotamuses. And all the while the artillery was booming with continuous, deafening roar.

Tom did not see the first of the boys to go over the top for they were over by the time he reached the second-line trench, but as he passed along the fire trench toward the road he could see them crowding over, and when he reached the road the barbed wire entanglements lay flat in many places, the boys picking their way across the fallen meshes, the clumsy tanks waddling on ahead, across No Man's Land. As far as Tom could see along the line in either direction this shell-torn area was being crossed by hundreds of boys in khaki holding fixed bayonets, some going ahead of the tanks and some perching on them.

Above him the whole district seemed to be in pandemonium, men shouting and their voices drowned by the thunder of artillery.

His first real sight of the attack was when he clambered out of the trench where it crossed the road and faced the flattened meshes of barbed wire with its splintered supporting poles all tangled in it. Never was there such a wreck.

"All right," he shouted down. "It's as flat as a pancake—careful with the machine—lift the back wheel—that's right!"

He could hardly hear his own voice for the noise, and the very earth seemed to shake under the heavy barrage fire which protected them. In one sweeping, hasty glance he saw scores of figures in khaki running like mad and disappearing into the enemy trenches beyond.

"Do you mean to let the wire rest on this?" he asked, as his machine was lifted up and the first of the wire carriers came scrambling up after it; "it might get short-circuited."

"We'll run it over the poles, only hurry," the men answered.

They were evidently the very last of the advancing force, and even as Tom looked across the shell-torn area of No Man's Land, he could see the men picking their way over the

flattened entanglements and pouring into the enemy trenches. The tanks had already crossed these and were rearing
and waddling along, irresistible yet ridiculous, like so many
heroic mud turtles going forth to glory. Here and there Tom
could see the gray-clad form of a German clambering out of
the trenches and rushing pell-mell to the rear.

But it was no time to stand and look. Hurriedly they
disentangled a couple of the supporting poles, laying them so
that the telephone wire passed over them free of the barbed
meshes and Tom, mounting his machine, started at top speed
along the road across No Man's Land, dragging the wire after
him. Scarcely had he started when he heard that wasplike
whizzing close to him—once, twice, and then a sharp
metallic sound as a bullet hit some part of his machine. He
looked back to see if the wire carriers were following, but
there was not a sign of any of them except his companion
who carried the apparatus, and just as Tom looked this man
twirled around like a top, staggered, and fell.

The last of the Americans were picking their way across the
tangle of fallen wire before the German fire trench. He could
see them now and again amid dense clouds of smoke as they
scrambled over the enemy sandbags and disappeared.

On he sped at top speed, not daring to look around again. He
could feel that the wire was dragging and he wondered
where its supporters could be; but he opened his cut-out to
get every last bit of power and sped on with the accumu-
lating train of wire becoming a dead weight behind him.

Now, far ahead, he could see gray-coated figures scrambling
frantically out of the first line trench, and he thought that the
Americans must have carried the attack successfully that far,
in any event. Again came that whizzing sound close to him,
and still again a sharp metallic ring as another bullet struck

his machine. For a moment he feared least a tire had been punctured, but when neither collapsed he took fresh courage and sped on.

The drag on the wire was lessening the speed of his machine now and jerking dangerously at intervals. But he thought of what one of those soldiers had said banteringly to another— *Stick around at the other end of it and listen to what you hear*, and he was resolved that if limited horse power and unlimited will power could get this wire to those brave boys who were surging and battling in the trenches ahead of him, could drag it to them wherever they went, for the glorious message they intended to send back across it, it should be done.

There was not another soul visible on that road now nor in the shell-torn area of No Man's Land through which it ran. But the lone rider forged ahead, zig-zagging his course to escape the bullets of that unseen sharpshooter and because it seemed to free the dragging, catching wire, affording him little spurts of unobstructed speed.

Then suddenly the wire caught fast, and his machine stopped and strained like a restive horse, the power wheel racing furiously. Hurriedly he looked behind him where the sinuous wire lay along the road, far back—as far as he could see, across the trampled entanglements and trenches. Where were the others who were to help carry it over? Killed?

Alone in the open area of No Man's Land, Tom Slade paused for an instant to think. What should he do?

Suddenly there appeared out of a shell hole not twenty feet ahead of him a helmeted figure. It rose up grimly, uncannily, like a dragon out of the sea, and levelled a rifle straight at him. So that was the lair of the sharpshooter!

Tom was not afraid. He knew that he had been facing death and he was not afraid of what he had been facing. He knew that the sharpshooter had him at last. Neither he nor the wire were going to bear any message back.

"Anyway, I'm glad I wrote that letter," he muttered.

CHAPTER SEVEN

A SHOT

Then, clear and crisp against the sound of the great guns far off, there was the sharp crack of a rifle and Tom was surprised to find himself still standing by his machine uninjured, while the Boche collapsed back into his shell hole like a jack-in-the-box.

He did not pause to think now. Leaving his machine, he rushed pell-mell back to the barbed wire entanglement where the line was caught, disengaged it and ran forward again to his wheel. Shells were bursting all about him, but as he mounted he could see two figures emerge, one after the other, from the American trench where it crossed the road, and take up the burden of wire. He could feel the relief as he mounted and rode forward and it lightened his heart as well as his load. What had happened to delay the carriers he did not know. Perhaps those who followed him now were new ones and his former companions lay dead or wounded within their own lines. What he thought of most of all was his extraordinary escape from the Boche sharpshooter and he wondered who and where his deliverer could be.

He avoided looking into the shell hole as he passed it and soon he reached the enemy entanglements which the tanks had flattened. Even the flat meshes had been cleared from the road and here several regulars waited to help him. They were covered with dirt and looked as if they had seen action.

"Bully for you, kid!" one of them said, slapping Tom on the shoulder.

"You're all right, Towhead!"

"Lift the machine," said Tom; "they always put broken glass in the roads. I thought maybe they'd punctured my tire out there."

"They came near puncturing *you*, all right! What's your name?"

"Thatchy is mostly what I get called. My motorcycle is named *Uncle Sam*. Did you win yet?"

For answer they laughed and slapped him on the shoulder and repeated, "You're all right, kid!"

"Looks as if Snipy must have had his eye on you, huh?" one of them observed.

"Who's Snipy?" Tom asked.

"Oh, that's mostly what *he* gets called," said someone, mimicking Tom's own phrase. "His rifle's named *Tommy*. He's probably up in a tree somewheres out there."

"He's a good shot," said Tom simply. "I'd like to see him."

"Nobody ever sees him—they *feel* him," said another.

"He must have been somewhere," said Tom.

Percy Keese Fitzhugh

"Oh, he was *somewhere* all right," several laughed.

A couple of the Signal Corps men jumped out of the trench near by and greeted Tom heartily, praising him as the others had done, all of which he took with his usual stolidness. Already, though of course he did not know it, he was becoming somewhat of a character.

"You've got Paul Revere and Phil Sheridan beat a mile," one of the boys said.

"I don't know much about Sheridan," said Tom, "but I always liked Paul Revere."

He did not seem to understand why they laughed and clapped him on the shoulder and said, "You'll do, kiddo."

But it was necessary to keep moving, for the other carriers were coming along. The little group passed up the road, Tom pushing his wheel and answering their questions briefly and soberly as he always did. Planks had been laid across the German trenches where they intersected the road and as they passed over them Tom looked down upon many a gruesome sight which evidenced the surprise by the Americans and their undoubted victory. Not a live German was to be seen, nor a dead American either, but here and there a fallen gray-coat lay sprawled in the crooked topsy-turvy ditch. He could see the Red Cross stretcher-bearers passing in and out of the communication trenches and already a number of boys in grimy khaki were engaged in repairing the trenches where the tanks had caved them in. In the second line trench lay several wounded Americans and Tom was surprised to see one of these propped up smoking a cigarette while the surgeons bandaged his head until it looked like a great white ball. Out of the huge bandage a white face grinned up as the little group passed across on the planks and seeing the men to be wire carriers, the wounded soldier called, "Tell 'em we're here."

"Ever hear of Paul Revere?" one of the Signal men called back cheerily. And he rumpled Tom's hair to indicate whom he meant.

Thus it was that Thatchy acquired the new nickname by which he was to be known far and wide in the country back of the lines and in the billet villages where he was to sit, his trusty motorcycle close at hand, waiting for messages and standing no end of jollying. Some of the more resourceful wits in khaki even parodied the famous poem for his benefit, but he didn't care. He would have matched *Uncle Sam* against Paul Revere's gallant steed any day, and they could jolly him and "kid" him as their mood prompted, but woe be to the person who touched his faithful machine save in his watchful presence. Even General Pershing would not have been permitted to do that.

CHAPTER EIGHT

IN THE WOODS

Beyond the enemy second line trench the road led straight into Cantigny and Tom could see the houses in the distance. Continuous firing was to be heard there and he supposed that the Germans, routed from their trenches, were making a stand in the village and in the high ground beyond it.

"They'll be able to 'phone back, won't they?" he asked anxiously.

"They sure will," one of the men answered.

"It ain't that I don't want to ride back," Tom explained, "but a feller's waiting on the other end of this wire, 'cause I heard somebody tell him to, and I wouldn't want him to be disappointed."

"He won't be disappointed."

The road, as well as the open country east and west of it, was strewn with German dead and wounded, among whom Tom saw one or two figures in khaki. The Red Cross was busy here, many stretchers being borne up toward the village where dressing stations were already being established. Then suddenly Tom beheld a sight which sent a thrill through him. Far along the road, in the first glare of the rising sun, flew the Stars and Stripes above a little cottage within the confines of the village.

"Headquarters," one of his companions said, laconically.

"Does it mean we've won?" Tom asked.

"Not exactly yet," the other answered, "but as long as the flag's up they probably won't bother to take it down," and he looked at Tom in a queer way. "There's cleaning up to do yet, kid," he added.

As they approached the village the hand-to-hand fighting was nearing its end, and the Germans were withdrawing into the woods beyond where they had many machine gun nests which it would be the final work of the Americans to smoke out. But Tom saw a little of that kind of warfare which is fought in streets, from house to house, and in shaded village greens. Singly and in little groups the Americans sought out, killing, capturing and pursuing the diminishing horde of Germans. Two of these, running frantically with apparently no definite purpose, surrendered to Tom's group and he thought they seemed actually relieved.

At last they reached the little cottage where the flag flew and were received by the weary, but elated, men in charge.

"All over but the shouting," someone said; "we're finishing up back there in the woods."

The telephone apparatus was fastened to a tree and Tom heard the words of the speaker as he tried to get into com-munication with the village which lay back across that shell-torn, trench-crossed area which they had traversed. At last he heard those thrilling words which carried much farther than the length of the sinuous wire:

"Hello, this is Cantigny."

And he knew that whatever yet remained to be done, the first real offensive operation of the Americans was successful and he was proud to feel that he had played his little part in it.

He was given leave until three o'clock in the afternoon and, leaving *Uncle Sam* at the little makeshift headquarters, he went about the town for a sight of the "clean-up."

Farther back in the woods he could still hear the shooting where the Americans were searching out machine gun nests and the boom of artillery continued, but although an occasional shell fell in the town, the place was quiet and even peaceful by comparison with the bloody clamor of an hour before.

It seemed strange that he, Tom Slade, should be strolling about this quaint, war-scarred village, which but a little while before had belonged to the Germans. Here and there in the streets he met sentinels and occasionally an airplane sailed overhead. How he envied the men in those airplanes!

He glanced in through broken windows at the interiors of simple abodes which the bestial Huns had devastated. It thrilled him that the boys from America had dragged and driven the enemy out of these homes and would dig their protecting trenches around the other side of this stricken village, like a great embracing arm. It stirred him to think that it was now within the refuge of the American lines and that the arrogant Prussian officers could no longer defile those low, raftered rooms.

He inquired of a sentinel where he could get some gasoline which he would need later.

"There's a supply station along that road," the man said; "just beyond the clearing."

Tom turned in that direction. The road took him out of the village and through a little clump of woods to a clearing where several Americans were guarding a couple of big gasoline tanks—part of the spoils of war. He lingered for a few minutes and then strolled on toward the edge of the denser wood beyond where the firing, though less frequent, could still be heard.

He intended to go just far enough into this wood for a glimpse of the forest shade which his scouting had taught him to love, and then to return to headquarters for his machine.

Crossing a plank bridge across a narrow stream, he paused in the edge of the woods and listened to the firing which still occurred at intervals in the higher ground beyond. He knew that the fighting there was of the old-fashioned sort, from behind protecting trees and wooded hillocks, something like the good old fights of Indians and buckskin scouts away home in the wild west of America. And he could not repress his impulse to venture farther into the solitude.

The stream which he had crossed had evidently its source in the more densely wooded hills beyond and he followed it on its narrowing way up toward the locality where the fighting seemed now to be going on. Once a group of khaki-clad figures passed stealthily among the trees, intent upon some quest. The sight of their rifles reminded Tom that he was himself in danger, but he reflected that he was in no greater danger than they and that he had with him the small arm which all messengers carried.

Percy Keese Fitzhugh

A little farther on he espied an American concealed behind a tree, who nodded his head perfunctorily as Tom passed, seeming to discourage any spoken greeting.

The path of the stream led into an area of thick undergrowth covering the side of a gentle slope where the water tumbled down in little falls. He must be approaching very near to the source, he thought, for the stream was becoming a mere trickle, picking its way around rocky obstacles in a very jungle of thick underbrush.

Suddenly he stopped at a slight rustling sound very near him.

It was the familiar sound which he had so often heard away back in the Adirondack woods, of some startled creature scurrying to shelter.

He was the scout again now, standing motionless and silent —keenly waiting. Then, to his amazement, a clump of bushes almost at his feet stirred slightly. He waited still, watching, his heart in his mouth. Could it have been the breeze? But there was no breeze.

Startled, but discreetly motionless, he fixed his eyes upon the leafy clump, still waiting. Presently it stirred again, very perceptibly now, then moved, clumsily and uncannily, and with a slight rustling of its leaves, along the bank of the stream!

CHAPTER NINE

THE MYSTERIOUS FUGITIVE

Suddenly the thing stopped, and its whole bulk was shaken very noticeably. Then a head emerged from it and before Tom could realize what had happened a German soldier was fully revealed, brushing the leaves and dirt from his gray coat as he stole cautiously along the edge of the stream, peering anxiously about him and pausing now and again to listen.

He was already some distance from Tom, whom apparently he had not discovered, and his stealthy movements suggested that he was either in the act of escaping or was bent upon some secret business of importance.

Without a sound Tom slipped behind a tree and watched the man who paused like a startled animal at every few steps, watching and listening.

Tom knew that, notwithstanding his non-combatant status, he was quite justified in drawing his pistol upon this fleeing Boche, but before he had realized this the figure had gone too far to afford him much hope of success with the small weapon which he was not accustomed to. Moreover, just because he *was* a "non-com" he balked at using it. If he should miss, he thought, the man might turn upon him and with a surer aim lay him low.

But there was one thing in which Tom Slade felt himself to be the equal of any German that lived, and that was stalking. Here, in the deep woods, among these protecting trees, he felt at home, and the lure of scouting was upon him now. No one could lose him; no one could get away from him. And a bird in the air would make no more noise than he!

Swiftly, silently, he slipped from one tree to another, his keen eye always fixed upon the fleeting figure and his ears alert to learn if, perchance, the Boche was being pursued. Not a sound could he hear except that of the distant shooting.

It occurred to him that the precaution of camouflaging might be useful to him also, and he silently disposed one of the leafy boughs which the German had left diagonally across his breast with the fork over his shoulder so that it formed a sort of adjustable screen, more portable and less clumsy than the leafy mound which had covered the Boche.

With this he stole along, sometimes hiding behind trees, sometimes crouching among the rocks along the bank, and keeping at an even distance from the man. His method with its personal dexterity was eloquent of the American scout, just as the Boche, under his mound of foliage, had been typical of the German who depends largely upon *device* and little upon personal skill and dexterity.

The scout from Temple Camp had his ruses, too, for once when the German, startled by a fancied sound, seemed about to look behind him, Tom dexterously hurled a stone far to the left of his quarry, which diverted the man's attention to that direction and kept it there while Tom, gliding this way and that and raising or lowering his scant disguise, crept after him.

They were now in an isolated spot and the distant firing seemed farther and farther away. The stream, reduced to a mere trickle, worked its way down among rocks and the German followed its course closely. What he was about in this sequestered jungle Tom could not imagine, unless, indeed, he was fleeing from his own masters. But surely open surrender to the Americans would have been safer than that, and Tom remembered how readily those other German soldiers had rushed into the arms of himself and his companions.

Moreover, the more overgrown the brook became and the more involved its path, the more the hurrying German seemed bent upon following it and instead of finding any measure of relief from anxiety in this isolated place, he appeared more anxious than ever and peered carefully about him at every few steps.

At length, to Tom's astonishment, he stepped across the brook and felt of a clump of bush which grew on the bank. Could he have expected to find another camouflaged figure, Tom wondered?

Whatever he was after, he apparently thought he had reached his destination for he now moved hurriedly about, feeling the single bushes and moving among the larger clumps as if in quest of something. After a few moments he paused as if perplexed and moved farther up the stream. And Tom, who had been crouching behind a bush at a safe distance, crept silently to another one, greatly puzzled but watching him closely.

Selecting another spot, the Boche moved about among the bushes as before, carefully examining each one which stood by itself. Tom expected every minute to see some grim, gray-coated figure step out of his leafy retreat to join his comrade, but why such a person should wait to be discovered Tom could not comprehend, for he must have heard and probably seen this beating through the bushes.

An especially symmetrical bush stood on the brink of the stream and after poking about this as usual, the German stood upon tiptoe, apparently looking down into it, then kneeled at its base while Tom watched from his hiding-place.

Suddenly a sharp report rang out and the German jumped to his feet, clutched frantically at the brush which seemed to furnish a substantial support, then reeled away and fell headlong into the brook, where he lay motionless.

The heedless current, adapting itself readily to this grim obstruction, bubbled gaily around the gray, crumpled form, accelerating its cheery progress in the narrow path and showing little glints of red in its crystal, dancing ripples.

CHAPTER TEN

THE JERSEY SNIPE

Tom hurried to the prostrate figure and saw that the German was quite dead. There was no other sign of human presence and not a sound to be heard but the rippling of the clear water at his feet.

For a few moments he stood, surprised and silent, listening. Then he fancied that he heard a rustling in the bushes some distance away and he looked in that direction, standing motionless, alert for the slightest stir.

Suddenly there emerged out of the undergrowth a hundred or more feet distant a strange looking figure clad in a dull shade of green with a green skull cap and a green scarf, like a scout scarf, loosely thrown about his neck. Even the rifle which he carried jauntily over his shoulder was green in color, so that he seemed to Tom to have that general hue which things assume when seen through green spectacles. He was lithe and agile, gliding through the bushes as if he were a part of them, and he came straight toward Tom, with a nimbleness which almost rivalled that of a squirrel.

There was something about his jaunty, light step which puzzled Tom and he narrowed his eyes, watching the

Percy Keese Fitzhugh

approaching figure closely. The stranger removed a cigarette from his mouth to enable him the better to lay his finger upon his lips, imposing silence, and as he did so the movement of his hand and his way of holding the cigarette somehow caused Tom to stare.

Then his puzzled scrutiny gave way to an expression of blank amazement, as again the figure raised his finger to his lips to anticipate any impulse of Tom's to call. Nor did Tom violate this caution until the stranger was within a dozen feet or so.

"Roscoe—Bent!" he ejaculated. "Don't you know me? I'm Tom Slade."

"Well—I'll—be—" Roscoe began, then broke off, holding Tom at arm's length and looking at him incredulously. "Tom Slade—*I'll be—jiggered*!"

"I kinder knew it was you," said Tom in his impassive way, "as soon as I saw you take that cigarette out of your mouth, 'cause you do it such a swell way, kind of," he added, ingenuously; "just like the way you used to when you sat on the window-sill in Temple Camp office and jollied Margaret Ellison. Maybe you don't remember."

Still Roscoe held him at arm's length, smiling all over his handsome, vivacious face. Then he removed one of his hands from Tom's shoulder and gave him a push in the chest in the old way.

"It's the same old Tom Slade, I'll be—And with the front of your belt away around at the side, as usual. This is better than taking a hundred prisoners. How are you and how'd you get here, you sober old tow-head, you?" and he gripped Tom's hand with impulsive vehemence. "This sure does beat all! I might have known if I found you at all it would be in the woods, you old pathfinder!" and he gave Tom another shove, then rapped him on the shoulder and slipped his hand around his neck in a way all his own.

"I—I like to hear you talk that way," said Tom, with that queer dullness which Roscoe liked; "it reminds me of old times."

"Kind of?" prompted Roscoe, laughing. "Is our friend here dead?"

"Yes, he's very dead," said Tom soberly, "but I think there are others around in the bushes."

"There are some enemies there," said Roscoe, "but we won't kill them. Contemptible murderers!" he muttered, as he hauled the dead Boche out of the stream. "I'll pick you off one by one, as fast as you come up here, you gang of back-stabbers! Look here," he added.

"I got to admit you can do it," said Tom with frank admiration.

Roscoe pulled away the shrubbery where the German had been kneeling when he was struck and there was revealed a great hogshead, larger, Tom thought, than any he had ever seen.

"That's the kind of weapons they fight with," Roscoe said, disgustedly. "Look here," he added, pulling the foliage away still more. "Don't touch it. See? It leads down from another one. It's poison."

Tom, staring, understood well enough now, and he peered into the bushes about him in amazement as he heard

Roscoe say,

"Arsenic, the sneaky beasts."

"See what he was going to do?" he added, startling Tom out of his silent wondering. "There's half a dozen or more of these hogsheads in those bushes. As fast as this one empties it fills up again from another that stands higher. There's a whole nest of them here. See how the pipe from this one leads into the stream?"

"What's the wire for?" said Tom.

"Oh, that's so's they can open this little cock here, see? Start the thing going. Don't pull away the camouflage. There may be another chap up here in a little while, to see what's the matter. *Tommy'll* take care of them all right, won't you, *Tommy*?"

"Do you mean me?" Tom asked.

"I mean your namesake here," Roscoe said, slapping his rifle. "I named it after you, you old glum head. Remember how you told me a feller couldn't aim straight, *kind of*" (he mimicked Tom's tone). "You said a feller couldn't aim straight, *kind of*, if he smoked cigarettes."

"I got to admit I was wrong," said Tom.

"You bet you have! Jingoes, it's good to hear you talk!" Roscoe laughed. "How in the world did you get here, anyway?"

"I'll tell you all about it," said Tom, "only first tell me, are you the feller they call the Jersey Snipe?"

"Snipy, for short," said Roscoe.

"Then maybe you saved my life already," said Tom, "out in No Man's Land."

"Were you the kid on that wheel?" Roscoe asked, surprised.

"Yes, and I always knew you'd make a good soldier. I told everybody so."

"*Kind of?* Tommy, old boy, don't forget it was *you* made me a soldier," Roscoe said soberly. "Come on back to my perch with me," he added, "and tell me all about your adventures. This is better than taking Berlin. There's only one person in this little old world I'd rather meet in a lonely place, and that's the Kaiser. Come on—quiet now."

"You don't think you can show *me* how to stalk, do you?" said Tom.

Percy Keese Fitzhugh

CHAPTER ELEVEN

ON GUARD

"You see it was this way," said Roscoe after hie had scrambled with amazing agility up to his "perch" in a tree several hundred feet distant but in full view of the stream. Tom had climbed up after him and was looking with curious pleasure at the little kit of rations and other personal paraphernalia which hung from neighboring branches. "How do you like my private camp? Got Temple Camp beat, hey?" he broke off in that erratic way of his. "All the comforts of home. Come on, get into your camouflage."

"You don't seem the same as when you used to come up to our office from the bank downstairs—that's one sure thing," said Tom, pulling the leaves about him.

"You thought all I was good for was to jolly Margaret Ellison, huh?"

"I see now that you didn't only save my life but lots of other fellers', too," said Tom. "Go on, you started to tell me about it."

It was very pleasant and cosy up there in the sniper's perch where Roscoe had gathered the thinner branches about him, forming a little leafy lair, in which his agile figure and his quick glances about reminded Tom for all the world of a squirrel. He could hardly believe that this watchful, dexterous creature, peering cautiously out of his romantic retreat, was the same Roscoe Bent who used to make fun of the scouts and sneak upstairs to smoke cigarettes in the Temple Camp office; who thought as much of his spotless high collar then as he seemed to think of his rifle now.

"I got to thank you because you named it after me," said Tom.

"And I *got to thank you* that you gave me the chance to get it to name after you, Tommy. Well, you see it was this way," Roscoe went on in a half whisper; "there were half a dozen of us over here in the woods and we'd just cleaned out a machine gun nest when we saw this miniature forest moving along. I thought it was a decorated moving van."

"That's the trouble with them," agreed Tom; "they're no good in the woods; they're clumsy. They're punk scouts."

"Scouts!" Roscoe chuckled. "If we had to fight this gang of cut-throats and murderers in the woods where old What's-his-name—Custer—had to fight the Indians, take it from me, we'd have them wiped up in a month. That fellow's idea of camouflaging was to bury himself under a couple of tons of green stuff and then move the whole business along like a clumsy old Zeppelin. I can camouflage myself with a branch with ten leaves on it by studying the light."

"Anybody can see you've learned something about scouting —that's one sure thing," said Tom proudly.

"*One sure thing!*" Roscoe laughed inaudibly. "It's the same old Tommy Slade. Well, I was just going to bean this geezer when my officer told me I'd better follow him."

"I was following him, too," said Tom; "stalking is the word you ought to use."

"Captain thought he might be up to something special. So I followed—*stalked*—how's that?"

"All right."

"So I stalked him and when I saw he was following the stream I made a detour and waited for him right here. You see what he was up to? Way down in Cantigny they could turn a switch and start this blamed poison, half a dozen hogsheads of it, flowing into the stream. They waited till they lost the town before they turned the switch, and they probably thought they could poison us Americans by wholesale. Maybe they had some reason to think the blamed thing hadn't worked, and sent this fellow up. I beaned him just as he was going to turn the stop-cock."

"Maybe you saved a whole lot of lives, hey?" said Tom proudly.

Roscoe shrugged his shoulder in that careless way he had. "I'll be glad to meet any more that come along," he said.

It was well that Tom Slade's first sight of deliberate killing was in connection with so despicable a proceeding as the wholesale poisoning of a stream. He could feel no pity for the man who, fleeing from those who fought cleanly and like men instead of beasts, had sought to pour this potent liquid of anguish and death into the running crystal water. Such acts, it seemed to him, were quite removed from the sphere of honorable, manly fighting.

As a scout he had learned that it was wrong even to bathe in a stream whence drinking water was obtained, and at camp he had always scrupulously observed this good rule. He felt that it was cowardly to defile the waters of a brook. It was not a "mailed fist" at all which could do such things, but a fist dripping with poison.

And Tom Slade felt no qualm, as otherwise he might have felt, at hiding there waiting for new victims. He was proud and thrilled to see his friend, secreted in his perch, keen-eyed and alert, guarding alone the crystal purity of this laughing, life-giving brook, as it hurried along its pebbly bed and tumbled in little gushing falls and wound cheerily around the rocks, bearing its grateful refreshment to the weary, thirsty boys who were holding the neighboring village.

"I used to think I wouldn't like to be a sniper," he said, "but now it seems different. I saw two fellers in the village and one had a bandage on his arm and the other one who was talking to him—I heard him say a long drink of water would go good—and—I—kind of—now—"

The Jersey Snipe winked at Tom and patted his rifle as a man might pat a favorite dog.

"It's good fresh water," said he.

CHAPTER TWELVE

WHAT'S IN A NAME?

In Tom's visions of the great war there had been no picture of the sniper, that single remnant of romantic and adventurous warfare, in all the roar and clangor of the horrible modern fighting apparatus.

He had seen American boys herded onto great ships by thousands; and, marching and eating and drilling in thousands, they had seemed like a great machine. He knew the murderous submarine, the aeroplane with its ear-splitting whir, the big clumsy Zeppelin; and he had handled gas masks and grenades and poison gas bombs.

But in his thoughts of the war and all these diabolical agents of wholesale death there had been no visions of the quiet, stealthy figure, inconspicuous in the counterfeiting hues of tree and rock, stealing silently away with his trusty rifle and his week's rations for a lonely vigil in some sequestered spot.

There was the same attraction about this freelance warfare which there might have been about a privateer in contrast with a flotilla of modern dreadnaughts and frantic chasers, and it reminded him of Daniel Boone, and Kit Carson, and Davy Crockett, and other redoubtable scouts of old who did not depend on stenching suffocation and the poisoning of streams. It was odd that he had never known much about the sniper, that one instrumentality of the war who seems to have been able to preserve a romantic identity in all the bloody *melee* of the mighty conflict.

For Tom had been a scout and the arts of stealth and concealment and nature's resourceful disguises had been his. He had thought of the sniper as of one whose shooting is done peculiarly in cold blood, and he was surprised and pleased to find his friend in this romantic and noble role of holding back, single-handed, as it were, these vile agents of agonizing death.

Arsenic! Tom knew from his memorized list of poison antidotes that if one drinks arsenic he will be seized with agony unspeakable and die in slow and utter torture. The more he thought about it, the more the cold, steady eye of the unseen sniper and his felling shot seemed noble and heroic.

Almost unconsciously he reached out and patted the rifle also as if it were some trusted living thing—an ally.

"Did you really mean you named it after me—honest?" he asked.

Roscoe laughed again silently. "See?" he whispered, holding it across, and Tom could distinguish the crudely engraved letters, TOMMY.

"—Because I never had anything named after me," he said in his simple, dull way. "There's a place on the lake up at Temple Camp that the fellers named after Roy Blakeley— Blakeley Isle. And there's a new pavilion up there that's named after Mr. Ellsworth, our scoutmaster. And Mr. Temple's got lots of things—orphan asylums and gymnasiums and buildings and things—named after *him*. I always thought it must be fine. I ain't that kind—sort of—that fellers name things after," he added, with a blunt simplicity that went to Roscoe's heart; and he held the rifle, as the sniper started to take it back, his eyes still fixed upon the rough scratches which formed his own name. "In Bridgeboro there was a place in Barrell Alley," he went on, apparently without feeling, "where my father fell down one night when he was—when he'd had too much to drink, and after that everybody down there called it Slade's Hole. When I got in with the scouts, I didn't like it—kind of—"

Roscoe looked straight at Tom with a look as sure and steady as his rifle. "Slade's Hole isn't known outside of Barrell Alley, Tom," he said impressively, although in the same cautious undertone, "but *Tom Slade* is known from one end of this sector to the other."

"Thatchy's what they called me in Toul sector, 'cause my hair's always mussed up, I s'pose, and—"

"The first time I ever saw you to really know you, Tom, your hair was all mussed up—and I hope it'll always stay that way. That was when you came up there in the woods and made me promise to go back and register."

"I knew you'd go back 'cause—"

"I went back with bells on, and here I am. And here's *Tom Slade* that's stuck by me through this war. It's named *Tom Slade* because it makes good—see? Look here, I'll show you something else—you old hickory nut, you. See that," he added, pulling a small object from somewhere in his clothing.

Tom stared. "It's the Distinguished Service Cross," he said, his longing eyes fixed upon it.

"That's what it is. The old gent handed me that—if anybody should ask you."

Tom smiled, remembering Roscoe's familiar way of speaking of the dignified Mr. Temple, and of "Old Man" Burton, and "Pop" this and that.

"General Pershing?"

"The same. You've heard of him, haven't you? Very muchly, huh?"

"Why don't you wear it?" Tom asked.

"Why? Well, I'll tell you why. When your friend, Thatchy, followed me on that crazy trip of mine he borrowed some money for railroad fare, didn't he? And he had a Gold Cross that he used to get the money, huh? So I made up my mind that this little old souvenir from Uncle Samuel wouldn't hang on my distinguished breast till I got back and paid Tom Slade what I owed him and made sure that he'd got his own Cross safely back and was wearing it again. Do you get me?"

"I got my Cross back," said Tom, "and it's home. So you can put that on. You got to tell me how you got it, too. I always knew you'd make a success."

"It was *Tommy Slade* helped me to it, as usual. I beaned nine Germans out in No Man's Land, and got away slightly wounded—I stubbed my toe. Old Pop Clemenceau gave me a kiss and the old gent slipped me this for good luck," Roscoe said, pinning on the Cross to please Tom. "When Clemmy saw the name on the rifle, he asked what it meant and I told him it was named after a pal of mine back home in the U.S.A.—Tom Slade. Little I knew you were waltzing around the war zone on that thing of yours. I almost laughed in his face when he said, 'M'soo Tommee should be proud.'"

So the Premier of France had spoken the name of Tom Slade, whose father had had a mud hole in Barrell Alley named after him.

"I *am* proud," he stammered; "that's one sure thing. I'm proud on account of you—I am."

CHAPTER THIRTEEN

THE FOUNTAINS OF DESTRUCTION

As Tom had the balance of the day to himself he cherished but one thought—that of remaining with Roscoe as long as his leave would permit. If he had been in the woods up at Temple Camp, away back home in his beloved Catskills, he could hardly have felt more at home than he felt perched in this tree near the headwaters of the running stream; and to have Roscoe Bent crouching there beside him was more than his fondest dreams of doing his bit had pictured.

At short intervals they could hear firing, sometimes voices in the distance, and occasionally the boom of artillery, but except for these reminders of the fighting the scene was of that sort which Tom loved. It was there, while the sniper, all unseen, guarded the source of the stream, his keen eye alert for any stealthy approach, that Tom told him in hushed tones the story of his own experiences; how he had been a ship's boy on a transport, and had been taken aboard the German U-boat that had torpedoed her and held in a German prison camp, from which he and Archer had escaped and made their way through the Black Forest and across the Swiss border.

"Some kid!" commented Roscoe, admiringly; "the world ain't big enough for you, Tommy. If you were just back from

74   Percy Keese Fitzhugh

Mars I don't believe you'd be excited about it."

"Why should I be?" said literal Tom. "It was only because the feller I was with was born lucky; he always said so."

"Oh, yes, of course," said Roscoe sarcastically. "*I* say he was mighty lucky to be with *you.* Feel like eating?"

It was delightful to Tom sitting there in their leafy conceal-ment, waiting for any other hapless German emissaries who might come, bent on the murderous defilement of that crystal brook, and eating of the rations which Roscoe never failed to have with him.

"You're kind of like a pioneer," he said, "going off where there isn't anybody. They have to trust you to do what you think best a lot, I guess, don't they? A feller said they often hear you but they never see you. I saw you riding on one of the tanks, but I didn't know it was you. Funny, wasn't it?"

"I usually hook a ride. The tanks get on my nerves, though, they're so slow."

"You're like a squirrel," said Tom admiringly.

"Well, you're like a bulldog," said Roscoe. "Still got the same old scowl on your face, haven't you? So they kid you a lot, do they?"

"I don't mind it."

So they talked, in half whispers, always scanning the woods about them, until after some time their vigil was rewarded by the sight of three gray-coated, helmeted figures coming up the bank of the stream. They made no pretence of conceal-ment, evidently believing themselves to be safe here in the forest. Roscoe had hauled the body of the dead German under the thick brush so that it might not furnish a warning to other visitors, and now he brought his rifle into position and touching his finger to his lips by way of caution he fixed his steady eye on the approaching trio.

One of these was a tremendous man and, from his uniform and arrogant bearing, evidently an officer. The other two were plain, ordinary "Fritzies." Tom believed that they had come to this spot by some circuitous route, bent upon the act which their comrade and the mechanism had failed to accomplish. He watched them in suspense, glancing occasionally at Roscoe.

The German officer evidently knew the ground for he went straight to the bush where the hogshead stood concealed, and beckoned to his two underlings. Tom, not daring to stir, looked expectantly at Roscoe, whose rifle was aimed and resting across a convenient branch before him. The sniper's intent profile was a study. Tom wondered why he did not fire. He saw one of the Boches approach the officer, who evidently would not deign to stoop, and kneel at the foot of the bush. Then the crisp, echoing report of Roscoe's rifle rang out, and on the instant the officer and the remaining soldier disappeared behind the leaf-covered hogshead. Tom was aware of the one German lying beside the bush, stark and motionless, and of Roscoe jerking his head and screwing up his mouth in a sort of spontaneous vexation. Then he looked suddenly at Tom and winked unmirthfully with a kind of worried annoyance.

"Think they can hit us from there? Think they know where we are?" Tom asked in the faintest whisper.

"'Tisn't that," Roscoe whispered back. "Look at that flat stone under the bush there. Shh! I couldn't get him in the

Percy Keese Fitzhugh

right light before. Shh!"

Narrowing his eyes, Tom scanned the earth at the foot of the bush and was just able to discern a little band of black upon a gray stone there. It was evidently a wet spot on the dusty stone and for a second he thought it was blood; then the staggering truth dawned upon him that in shooting the Hun in the very act of letting loose the murderous liquid Roscoe had shot a hole in the hogshead and the potent poison was flowing out rapidly and down into the stream.

And just in that moment there flashed into Tom's mind the picture of that weary, perspiring boy in khaki down in captured Cantigny, who had mopped his forehead, saying, "A drink of water would go good now."

CHAPTER FOURTEEN

TOM USES HIS FIRST BULLET

It had been a pet saying of Tom's scoutmaster back in America that you should *wait long enough to make up your mind and not one second longer.*

Tom knew that the pressure of liquid above that fatal bullet hole near the bottom of the hogshead was great enough to send the poison fairly pouring out. He could not see this death-dealing stream, for it was hidden in the bush, but he knew that it would continue to pour forth until several of these great receptacles had been emptied and the running brook with its refreshing coolness had become an instrument of frightful death.

Safe behind the protecting bulk of the hogshead crouched the two surviving Germans, while Roscoe, covering the spot, kept his eyes riveted upon it for the first rash move of either of the pair. And meanwhile the poison poured out of the very bulwark that shielded them and into the swift-running stream.

"I don't think they've got us spotted," Tom whispered, moving cautiously toward the trunk of the tree; "the private had a rifle, didn't he?"

"What are you going to do?" Roscoe breathed.

"Stop up that hole. Give me a bullet, will you?"

"You're taking a big chance, Tom."

"I ain't thinking about that. Give me a bullet. All *you* got to do is keep those two covered."

With a silent dexterity which seemed singularly out of keeping with his rather heavy build, Tom shinnied down the side of the tree farthest from the brook, and lying almost prone upon the ground began wriggling his way through the sparse brush, quickening his progress now and again whenever the diverting roar of distant artillery or the closer report of rifles and machine guns enabled him to advance with less caution.

In a few minutes he reached the stream, apparently undiscovered, when suddenly he was startled by another rifle report, close at hand, and he lay flat, breathing in suspense.

It was simply that one of that pair had made the mistake so often made in the trenches of raising his head, and had paid the penalty.

Tom was just cautiously crossing the brook when he became aware of a frantic scramble in the bush and saw the German private rushing pell-mell through the thick undergrowth beyond, hiding himself in it as best he might and apparently trying to keep the bush-enshrouded hogshead between himself and the tree where the sniper was. Evidently he had discovered Roscoe's perch and, there being now no restraining authority, had decided on flight. It had been the officer's battle, not his, and he abandoned it as soon as the officer was shot. It was typical of the German system and of the total lack of individual spirit and resource of the poor wretches who fight for Kaiser Bill's glory.

Reaching the bush, Tom pulled away the leafy covering and saw that the poisonous liquid was pouring out of a clean bullet hole as he had suspected. He hurriedly wrapped a bit of the gauze bandage which he always carried around the bullet Roscoe had given him and forced it into the hole, wedging it tight with a rock. Then he waved his hand in the direction of the tree to let Roscoe know that all was well.

Tom Slade had used his first bullet and it had saved hundreds of lives.

"They're both dead," he said, as Roscoe came quickly through the underbrush in the gathering dusk. "Did the officer put his head up?"

"Mm-mm," said Roscoe, examining the two victims.

"You always kill, don't you?" said Tom.

"I have to, Tommy. You see, I'm all alone, mostly," Roscoe added as he fumbled in the dead officer's clothing. "There are no surgeons or nurses in reach. I don't have stretcher-bearers following *me* around and it isn't often that even a Hun will surrender, fair and square, to one man. I've seen too much of this '*kamarad*' business. I can't afford to take chances, Tommy. But I don't put nicks in my rifle butt like some of them do. I don't want to know how many I beaned after it's all over. We kill to save—that's the idea you want to get into your head, Tommy boy."

"I know it," said Tom.

The officer had no papers of any importance and since it was

Percy Keese Fitzhugh

getting dark and Tom must report at headquarters, they discussed the possibility of upsetting these murderous hogsheads, and putting an end to the danger. Evidently the woods were not yet wholly cleared of the enemy who might still seek to make use of these agents of destruction.

"There may be stragglers in the woods even to-morrow," Roscoe said.

"S'pose we dig a little trench running away from the brook and then turn on the cock and let the stuff flow off?" suggested Tom.

The idea seemed a good one and they fell to, hewing out a ditch with a couple of sticks. It was a very crude piece of engineering, as Roscoe observed, and they were embarrassed in their work by the gathering darkness, but at length they succeeded, by dint of jabbing and plowing and lifting the earth out in handfuls, in excavating a little gully through the rising bank so that the liquid would flow off and down the rocky decline beyond at a safe distance from the stream.

For upwards of an hour they remained close by, until the hogsheads had run dry, and then they set out through the woods for the captured village.

CHAPTER FIFTEEN

THE GUN PIT

"I think the best way to get into the village," said Roscoe, "is to follow the edge of the wood around. That'll bring us to the by-path that runs into the main road. They've got the woods pretty well cleared out over that way. There's a road a little north of here and I think the Germans have withdrawn across that. What do you say?"

"You know more about it than I do," said Tom. "I followed the brook up. It's pretty bad in some places."

"There's only two of us," said Roscoe, "and you've no rifle. Safety first."

"I suppose there's a lot of places they could hide along the brook; the brush is pretty thick all the way up," Tom added.

Roscoe whistled softly in indecision. "I like the open better," said he.

"I guess so," Tom agreed, "when there's only two of us."

"There's three of us, though," said Roscoe, "and *Tommy* here likes the open better. I'd toss up a coin only with these blamed French coins you can't tell which is heads and which is tails."

Roscoe was right about the Germans having withdrawn beyond the road north of the woods. Whether he was right about its being safer to go around the edge of the forest remained to be determined.

This wood, in which they had passed the day, extended north of the village (see map) and thinned out upon the eastern side so that one following the eastern edge would emerge from the wood a little east of the main settlement. Here was the by-path which Roscoe had mentioned, and which led down into the main road.

Running east and west across the northern extremity of the woods was a road, and the Germans, driven first from their trenches, then out of the village, and then out of the woods, were establishing their lines north of this road.

If the boys had followed the brook down they would have reached the village by a much shorter course, but Roscoe preferred the open country where they could keep a better lookout. Whether his decision was a wise one, we shall see.

Leaving the scene of their "complete annihilation of the crack poison division," as Roscoe said, they followed the ragged edge of the woods where it thinned out to the north, verging around with it until they were headed in a southerly direction.

"There's a house on that path," said Roscoe, "and we ought to be able to see a light there pretty soon."

"There's a little piece of woods ahead of us," said Tom; "when we get past that we'll see it, I guess. We'll cut through there, hey?"

"Wait a minute," said Roscoe, pausing and peering about in the half darkness. "I'm all twisted. There's the house now."

He pointed to a dim light in the opposite direction to that which they had taken.

"That's north," said Tom in his usual dull manner.

"You're mistaken, my boy. What makes you think it's north?"

"I didn't say I thought so," said Tom. "I said it *is*."

Roscoe laughed. "Same old Tom," he said. "But how do you know it's north?"

"You remember that mountain up in the Catskills?" Tom said. "The first time I ever went to the top of that mountain was in the middle of the night. I never make that kind of mistakes. I know because I just know."

Roscoe laughed again and looked rather dubiously at the light in the distance. Then he shook his head, unconvinced.

"We've been winding in and out along the edge of this woods," said Tom, "so that you're kind of mixed up, that's all. It's always those little turns that throw people out, just like it's a choppy sea that upsets a boat; it ain't the big waves. I used to get rattled like that myself, but I don't any more."

Roscoe drew his lips tight and shook his head skeptically. "I can't understand about that light," he said.

"I always told you you made a mistake not to be a scout when you were younger," said Tom in that impassive tone

Percy Keese Fitzhugh

which seemed utterly free of the spirit of criticism and which always amused Roscoe, "'cause then you wouldn't bother about the light but you'd look at the stars. Those are sure."

Roscoe looked up at the sky and back at Tom, and perhaps he found a kind of reassurance in that stolid face. "All right, Tommy," said he, "what you say, goes. Come ahead."

"That light is probably on the road the Germans retreated across," said Tom, as they picked their way along. His unerring instinct left him entirely free from the doubts which Roscoe could not altogether dismiss. "I don't say there ain't a light on the path you're talking about, but if we followed this one we'd probably get captured. I was seven months in a German prison. I don't know how you'd like it, but I didn't."

Roscoe laughed silently at Tom's dry way of putting it. "All right, Tommy, boy," he said. "Have it your own way."

"You ought to be satisfied the way you can shoot," said Tom, by way of reconciling Roscoe to his leadership.

"All right, Tommy. Maybe you've got the bump of locality. When we get past that little arm of the woods just ahead we ought to see the right light then, huh?"

"*Spur* is the right name for it, not *arm*," said Tom. "You might as well say it right."

"The pleasure is mine," laughed Roscoe; "Tommy, you're as good as a circus."

They made their way in a southeasterly direction, following the edge of the woods, with the open country to the north and east of them. Presently they reached the "spur," as Tom called it, which seemed to consist of a little "cape" of woods, as one might say, sticking out eastward. They could shorten their path a trifle by cutting through here, and this they did, Roscoe (notwithstanding Tom's stolid self-confidence) watching anxiously for the light which this spur had probably concealed, and which would assure them that they were heading southward toward the path which led into Cantigny village.

Once, twice, in their passage through this little clump of woods Tom paused, examining the trees and ground, picking up small branches and looking at their ends, and throwing them away again.

"Funny how those branches got broken off," he said.

Roscoe answered with a touch of annoyance, the first he had shown since their meeting in the woods.

"I'm not worrying about those twigs," he said; "I don't see that light and I think we're headed wrong."

"They're not twigs," said Tom literally; "they're branches, and they're broken off."

"Any fool could tell the reason for that," said Roscoe, rather scornfully. "It's the artillery fire."

Tom said nothing, but he did not accept Roscoe's theory. He believed that some one had been through here before them and that the branches had been broken off by human hands; and but for the fact that Roscoe had let him have his own way in the matter of direction he would have suggested that they make a detour around this woody spur. However, he contented himself by saying in his impassive way, "I know when branches are broken off."

Percy Keese Fitzhugh

"Well, what are we going to do now?" Roscoe demanded, stopping short and speaking with undisguised impatience. "You can see far beyond those trees now and you can see there's no light. They'll have us nailed upon a couple of crosses to-morrow. I don't intend to be tortured on account of the Boy Scouts of America."

He used the name as being synonymous with bungling and silly notions and star-gazing, and it hit Tom in a dangerous spot. He answered with a kind of proud independence which he seldom showed.

"I didn't say there'd be a light. Just because there's a house it doesn't mean there's got to be a light. I said the light we saw was in the north, and it's got nothing to do with the Boy Scouts. You wouldn't let me point your rifle for you, would you? They sent me to this sector 'cause I don't get lost and I don't get rattled. You said that about the Scouts just because you're mad. I'm not hunting for any light. I'm going back to Cantigny and I know where I'm at. You can come if you want to or you can go and get caught by the Germans if you want to. I went a hundred miles through Germany and they didn't catch *me*—'cause I always know where I'm at."

He went on for a few steps, Roscoe, after the first shock of surprise, following silently behind him. He saw Tom stumble, struggle to regain his balance, heard a crunching sound, and then, to his consternation, saw him sink down and disappear before his very eyes.

In the same instant he was aware of a figure which was not Tom's scrambling up out of the dark, leaf-covered hollow and of the muzzle of a rifle pointed straight at him.

Evidently Tom Slade had not known "where he was at" at all.

CHAPTER SIXTEEN

PRISONERS

Apparently some of the enemy had not yet withdrawn to the north, for in less than five seconds Roscoe was surrounded by a group of German soldiers, among whom towered a huge officer with an eye so fierce and piercing that it was apparent even in the half darkness. He sported a moustache more aggressively terrible than that of Kaiser Bill himself and his demeanor was such as to make that of a roaring lion seem like a docile lamb by comparison. An Iron Cross depended from a heavy chain about his bull neck and his portly breast was so covered with the junk of rank and commemoration that it seemed like one of those boards from which street hawkers sell badges at a public celebration.

Poor Tom, who had been hauled out of the hole, stood dogged and sullen in the clutch of a Boche soldier, and Roscoe, even in his surprise at this singular turn of affairs, bestowed a look of withering scorn upon him.

"I knew those branches were *broken* off," Tom muttered, as if in answer. "They're using them for camouflage. It's got nothing to do with the other thing about which way we were going."

But Roscoe only looked at him with a sneer.

Wherever the wrong and right lay as to their direction, they had run plunk into a machine-gun nest and Roscoe Bent, with all his diabolical skill of aim, could not afford his fine indulgence of sneering, for as an active combatant, which Tom was not, he should have known that these nests were more likely to be found at the wood's edge than anywhere else, where they could command the open country. The little spur of woods afforded, indeed, an ideal spot for secreting a machine gun, whence a clear range might be had both north and south.

If Tom had not been a little afraid of Roscoe he would have acted on the good scout warning of the broken branches and made a detour in time to escape this dreadful plight. And the vain regret that he had not done so rankled in his breast now. The pit was completely surrounded and almost covered with branches, so that no part of the guns and their tripods which rose out of it was discoverable, at least to Roscoe.

"Vell, you go home, huh?" the officer demanded, with a grim touch of humor.

Roscoe was about to answer, but Tom took the words out of his mouth.

"We got lost and we got rattled," he said, with a frank confession which surprised Roscoe; "we thought we were headed south."

The sniper bestowed another angrily contemptuous look upon him, but Tom appeared not to notice it.

"Vell, we rattle you some more—vat?" the officer said, without very much meaning. His voice was enough to rattle any captive, but Tom was not easily disconcerted, and instead of cowering under this martial ferocity and the scorning looks of his friend, he glanced about him in his frowning, lowering way as if the surroundings interested him more than his captors. But he said nothing.

"You English—no?" the officer demanded.

"We're Americans," said Roscoe, regaining his self-possession.

"Ach! Diss iss good for you. If you are English, ve kill you! You have kamerads—vere?"

"There's only the two of us," said Roscoe. Tom seemed willing enough to let his companion do the talking, and indeed Roscoe, now that he had recovered his poise, seemed altogether the fitter of the two to be the spokesman. "We got rattled, as this kid says." "If we'd followed that light we wouldn't have happened in on you. We hope we don't intrude," he added sarcastically.

The officer glanced at the tiny light in the distance, then at one of the soldiers, then at another, then poured forth a gutteral torrent at them all. Then he peered suspiciously into the darkness.

"For treachery, ve kill," he said.

"I told you there are only two of us," said Roscoe simply.

"Ach, two! Two millions, you mean! Vat? Ach!" he added, with a deprecating wave of his hands. "Vy not *billions*, huh?"

Roscoe gathered that he was sneering skeptically about the number of Americans reported to be in France.

"Ve know just how many," the officer added; "vell, vat you got, huh?"

At this two of the Boches proceeded to search the captives, neither of whom had anything of value or importance about them, and handed the booty to the officer.

"Vat is diss, huh?" he said, looking at a small object in his hand.

Tom's answer nearly knocked Roscoe off his feet.

"It's a compass," said he.

So Tom had had a compass with him all the time they had been discussing which was the right direction to take! Why he had not brought it out to prove the accuracy of his own contention Roscoe could not comprehend.

"A compass, huh. Vy you not use it?"

"Because I was sure I was right," said Tom.

"Always sure you are right, you Yankees! Vat?"

"Nothing," said Tom.

The officer examined the trifling haul as well as he could in the darkness, then began talking in German to one of his men. And meanwhile Tom watched him in evident suspense, and Roscoe, unmollified, cast at Tom a look of sneering disgust for his bungling error—a look which seemed to include the whole brotherhood of scouts.

Finally the officer turned upon Roscoe with his characteristic martial ferocity.

"How long you in France?" he demanded.

"Oh, about a year or so."

"Vat ship you come on?"

"I don't know the name of it."

"You come to Havre, vat?"

"I didn't notice the port."

"Huh! You are not so—vide-avake, huh?"

"Absent-minded, yes," said Roscoe.

The officer paused, glaring at Roscoe, and Tom could not help envying his friend's easy and self-possessed air.

"You know the *Texas Pioneer*?" the officer shot out in that short, imperious tone of demand which is the only way in which a German knows how to ask a question.

"Never met him," said Roscoe.

"A ship!" thundered the officer.

"Oh, a ship. No, I've never been introduced."

"She come to Havre—vat?"

"That'll be nice," said Roscoe.

"You never hear of dis ship, huh?"

"No, there are so many, you know."

"To bring billions, yes!" the officer said ironically.

"That's the idea."

Pause.

"You hear about more doctors coming—no? Soon?"

"Sorry I can't oblige you," said Roscoe.

The officer paused a moment, glaring at him and Tom felt very unimportant and insignificant.

"Vell, anyway, you haf good muscle, huh?" the officer finally observed; then, turning to his subordinates, he held forth in German until it appeared to Tom that he and Roscoe were to carry the machine gun to the enemy line.

To Tom, under whose sullen, lowering manner, was a keenness of observation sometimes almost uncanny, it seemed that these men were not the regular crew which had been stationed here, but had themselves somehow chanced upon the deserted nest in the course of their withdrawal from the village.

For one thing, it seemed to him that this imperious officer was a personage of high rank, who would not ordinarily have been stationed in one of these machine gun pits. And for another thing, there was something (he could not tell exactly what) about the general demeanor of their captors, their way of removing the gun and their apparent unfamiliarity with the spot, which made him think that they had stumbled into it in the course of their wanderings just as he and Roscoe had done. They talked in German and he could not understand them, but he noticed particularly; that the two who went into the pit to gather the more valuable portion of the paraphernalia appeared not to be familiar with the place, and he thought that the officer inquired of them whether there were two or more guns.

When he lifted his share of the burden, Roscoe noticed how he watched the officer with a kind of apprehension, almost terror, in his furtive glance, and kept his eyes upon him as they started away in the darkness.

Roscoe was in a mood to think ill of Tom, whom he considered the bungling, stubborn author of their predicament. It pleased him now to believe that Tom was afraid and losing his nerve. He remembered that he had said they would be crucified as a result of Tom's pin-headed error. And he was rather glad to believe that Tom was thinking of that now.

CHAPTER SEVENTEEN

SHADES OF ARCHIBALD ARCHER

After a minute the officer paused and consulted with one of his men; then another was summoned to the confab, the three of them reminding Tom of a newspaper picture he had seen of the Kaiser standing in a field with two officers and gazing fiercely at a map.

One of the soldiers waved a hand toward the distance, while Tom watched sharply. And Roscoe, who accepted their predicament with a kind of reckless bravado, sneered slightly at Tom's evident apprehension.

Then the officer produced something, holding it in his hand while the others peered over his shoulder. And Tom watched them with lowering brows, breathing hurriedly. No one knew it, but in that little pause Tom Slade lived a whole life of nervous suspense. It was not, however, the nervousness and suspense which his friend thought.

Then, as if unable to control his impulse, he moved slightly as though to start in the direction which he and Roscoe had been following. It was only a slight movement, made in obedience to an overwhelming desire, and as if he would incline his captors' thoughts in that direction. Roscoe, who held his burden jointly with Tom, felt this impatient impulse communicated to him and he took it as a confession from Tom that he had made the fatal error of mistaking their way before. And he moved a trifle, too, in the direction where he knew the German lines had been established, muttering scornfully at Tom, "You know where you're headed for now, all right. It's what I said right along."

"I admit I know," said Tom dully.

No doubt it was the compass which was the main agent in deciding the officer as to their route, but he and his men moved, even as Tom did, as if to make an end of needless parleying.

As they tramped along, following the edge of the wood, a tiny light appeared ahead of them, far in the distance, like a volunteer beacon, and Roscoe, turning, a trifle puzzled, tried to discover the other light, which had now diminished to a mere speck. Now and again the officer paused and glanced at that trifling prize of war, Tom's little glassless, tin-encased compass. But Tom Slade of Temple Camp, Scout of the Circle and the Five Points, winner of the Acorn and the Indianhead, looked up from time to time at the quiet, trustful stars.

So they made their way along, following a fairly straight course, and verging away from the wood's edge, heading toward the distant light. Two of the Germans went ahead with fixed bayonets, scouring the underbrush, and the others escorted Tom and Roscoe, who carried all of the burden.

The officer strode midway between the advance guard and the escorting party, pausing now and again as if to make sure of his ground and occasionally consulting the compass. Once he looked up at the sky and then Tom fairly trembled. He might have saved himself this worry, however, for Herr Officer recognized no friends nor allies in that peaceful, gold-studded heaven.

"It was an unlucky day for me I ran into you over here," Roscoe muttered, yielding to his very worst mood.

Tom said nothing.

"We won't even have the satisfaction of dying in action now."

No answer.

"After almost a year of watching my step I come to this just because I took *your* word. Believe *me*, I deserve to hang. I don't even get on the casualty list, on account of you. You see what we're both up against now, through that bump of locality you're so proud of. Edwards' Grove[1] is where *you* belong. I'm not blaming you, though—I'm blaming myself for listening to a dispatch kid!"

The Germans, not understanding, paid no attention, and Roscoe went on, reminding Tom of the old, flippant, cheaply cynical Roscoe, who had stolen his employer's time to smoke cigarettes in the Temple Camp office, trying to arouse the stenographer's mirth by ridiculing the Boy Scouts.

"I'm not thinking about what you're saying," he said bluntly, after a few minutes. "I'm remembering how you saved my life and named your gun after me."

"Hey, Fritzie, have they got any Boy Scouts in Germany?" Roscoe asked, ignoring Tom, but speaking apparently at him. The nearest Boche gave a glowering look at the word *Fritzie*, but otherwise paid no attention.

"We were on our way to German headquarters, anyway," Roscoe added, addressing himself indifferently to the soldiers, "but we're glad of your company. The more, the merrier. Young Daniel Boone here was leading the way."

The Germans, of course, did not understand, but Tom felt ashamed of his companion's cynical bravado. The insults to himself he did not mind. His thoughts were fixed on something else.

On they went, into a marshy area where Tom looked more apprehensively at the officer than before, as if he feared the character of the ground might arouse the suspicion of his captors. But they passed through here without pause or question and soon were near enough to the flickering light to see that it burned in a house.

Again Roscoe looked perplexedly behind him, but the light there was not visible at all now. Again the officer stopped and, as Tom watched him fearfully, he glanced about and then looked again at the compass.

For one brief moment the huge figure stood there, outlined in the darkness as if doubting. And Tom, looking impassive and dogged, held his breath in an agony of suspense.

It was nothing and they moved on again, Roscoe, in complete repudiation of his better self, indulging his sullen anger and making Tom and the Scouts (as if they had anything to do with it) the victims of his cutting shafts.

And still again the big, medal-bespangled officer paused to look at the compass, glanced, suspiciously, Tom thought, at the faint shadow of a road ahead of them, and moved on, his medals clanging and chinking in unison with his martial stride.

Percy Keese Fitzhugh

And Tom Slade of Temple Camp, Scout of the Circle and the Five Points, winner of the Acorn and the Indianhead, glanced up from time to time at the quiet, trustful stars.

If he thought of any human being then, it was not of Roscoe Bent (not *this* Roscoe Bent, in any event), but of a certain young friend far away, he did not know where. And he thanked Archibald Archer, vandal though he was, for, one idle, foolish thing that he had done.

[1] The woods near Bridgeboro, in America, where Tom and the Scouts had hiked and camped.

CHAPTER EIGHTEEN

THE BIG COUP

No one knew, no one ever would know, of the anxiety and suspense which Tom Slade experienced in that fateful march through the country above Cantigny. Every uncertain pause of that huge officer, and every half inquiring turn of his head sent a shock of chill misgiving through poor Tom and he trudged along under the weight of his burden, hearing the flippant and bitter jibes of Roscoe as if in a trance.

At last, having crossed a large field, they fell into a well-worn path, and here Tom experienced his moment of keenest anxiety, for the officer paused as if in momentary recognition of the spot. For a second he seemed a bit perplexed, then strode on. Still again he paused within a few yards of the little house where the light had appeared.

But it was too late. About this house a dozen or more figures moved in the darkness. Their style of dress was not distinguishable, but Tom Slade called aloud to them, "Here's some prisoners we brought you back."

In an instant they were surrounded by Americans and Tom thought that his native tongue had never sounded so good before.

　　　　　Percy Keese Fitzhugh

"Hello, Snipy," some one said.

But Roscoe Bent was too astonished to answer. In a kind of trance he saw the big Prussian officer start back, heard him utter some terrific German expletive, beheld the others of the party herded together, and was aware of the young American captain giving orders. In a daze he looked at Tom's stolid face, then at the Prussian officer, who seemed too stunned to say anything after his first startled outburst. He saw two boys in khaki approaching with lanterns and in the dim light of these he could distinguish a dozen or so khaki-clad figures perched along a fence.

"Where are we at, anyway?" he finally managed to ask.

"Just inside the village," one of the Americans answered.

"What village?"

"Coney Island on the subway," one of the boys on the fence called.

"Cantigny," some one nearer to him said. "You made a good haul."

"Well—I'll—be—" Roscoe began.

Tom Slade said nothing. Like a trusty pilot leaving his ship he strolled over and vaulted up on the fence beside the boys who, having taken the village, were now making themselves comfortable in it. His first question showed his thought-fulness.

"Is the brook water all right?"

"Sure. Thirsty?"

"No, I only wanted to make sure it was all right. There were some big hogsheads of poison up in the woods where the brook starts and the other feller killed three Germans who tried to empty them in the stream. By mistake he shot a hole in one of the hogsheads and I thought maybe some of the stuff got into the water. But I guess it didn't."

It was characteristic of Tom that he did not mention his own part in the business.

"I drank about a quart of it around noontime," said a young sergeant, "and I'm here yet."

"It's good and cool," observed another.

"What's the matter with Snipy, anyway?" a private asked, laughing. "Somebody been spinning him around?"

"He just got mixed up, kind of, that's all," Tom said.

That was all.

There was much excitement in and about the little cottage on the edge of the village. Up the narrow path, from head-quarters below, came other Americans, officers as Tom could see, who disappeared inside the house. Presently, the German prisoners, all except the big officer, came out, sullen in captivity, poor losers as Germans always are, and marched away toward the centre of the village, under escort.

"They thought they were taking us to the German lines," said Tom simply.

Roscoe, having recovered somewhat from his surprise and feeling deeply chagrined, walked over and stood in front of Tom.

"Why didn't you show me that compass, Tom?" he asked.

"Because it was wrong, just like you were," Tom answered frankly, but without any trace of resentment. "If I'd showed it to you you'd have thought it proved you were right. It was marked, crazy like, by that feller I told you about. I knew all the time we were coming to Cantigny."

There was a moment of silence, then Roscoe, his voice full of feeling, said simply,

"Tom Slade, you're a wonder."

"Hear that, Paul Revere?" one of the soldiers said jokingly. "Praise from the Jersey Snipe means something."

"No, it don't either," Roscoe muttered in self-distrust. "You've saved me from a Hun prison camp and while you were doing it you had to listen to me—Gee! I feel like kicking myself," he broke off.

"I ain't blaming you," said Tom, in his expressionless way. "If I'd had my way we'd have made a detour when I saw those broken branches, 'cause I knew it meant people were there, and then we wouldn't have got those fellers as prisoners, at all. So they got to thank you more than me."

This was queer reasoning, indeed, but it was Tom Slade all over.

"Me!" said Roscoe, "that's the limit. Tom, you're the same old hickory nut. Forgive me, old man, if you can."

"I don't have to," said Tom.

Roscoe stood there staring at him, thrilled with honest

admiration and stung by humiliation.

And as the little group, augmented by other soldiers who strolled over to hear of this extraordinary affair first hand, grew into something of a crowd, Tom, alias Thatchy, alias Paul Revere, alias Towhead, sat upon the fence, answering questions and telling of his great coup with a dull unconcern which left them all gaping.

"As soon as I made up my mind they didn't belong there," he said, "I decided they weren't sure of their own way, kind of. If the big man hadn't taken the compass away from me, I'd have given it to him anyway. It had the N changed into an S and the S into an N. I think he kind of thought the other way was right, but when he saw the compass, that settled him. All the time I was looking at the Big Dipper, 'cause I knew nobody ever tampered with that. I noticed he never even looked up, but once, and then I was scared. When we got to the marsh, I was scared, too, 'cause I thought maybe he'd know about the low land being south of the woods. I was scared all the time, as you might say, but mostly when he turned his head and seemed kind of uncertain-like. It ain't so much any credit to me as it is to Archer—the feller that changed the letters. Anyway, I ain't mad, that's sure," he added, evidently intending this for Roscoe. "Everybody gets mistaken sometimes."

"You're one bully old trump, Tom," said Roscoe shame-facedly.

"So now you see how it was," Tom concluded. "I couldn't get rattled as long as I could see the Big Dipper up there in the sky."

For a few moments there was silence, save for the low whistling of one of the soldiers.

Percy Keese Fitzhugh

"You're all right, kiddo," he broke off to say.

Then one of the others turned suddenly, giving Tom a cordial rap on the shoulder which almost made him lose his balance. "Well, as long as we've got the Big Dipper," said he, "and as long as the water's pure, what d'you say we all go and have a drink—in honor of Paul Revere?"

So it was that presently Tom and Roscoe found themselves sitting alone upon the fence in the darkness. Neither spoke. In the distance they could hear the muffled boom of some isolated field-piece, belching forth its challenge in the night. High overhead there was a whirring, buzzing sound as a shadow glided through the sky where the stars shone peacefully. A company of boys in khaki, carrying internching implements, passed by, greeting them cheerily as they trudged back from doing their turn in digging the new trench line which would embrace Cantigny.

Cantigny!

"I'm glad we took the town, that's one sure thing," Tom said.

"It's the first good whack we've given them," agreed Roscoe.

Again there was silence. In the little house across the road a light burned. Little did Tom Slade know what was going on there, and what it would mean to him. And still the American boys guarding this approach down into the town, moved to and fro, to and fro, in the darkness.

"Tom," said Roscoe, "I was a fool again, just like I was before, back home in America. Will you try to forget it, old man?" he added.

"There ain't anything to forget," said Tom, "I got to be

thankful I found you; that's the only thing I'm thinking about and—and—that we didn't let the Germans get us. If you like a feller you don't mind about what he says. Do you think I forget you named that rifle after me? Just because—because you didn't know about trusting to the stars,—I wouldn't be mad at you—"

Roscoe did not answer.

CHAPTER NINETEEN

TOM IS QUESTIONED

When it became known in the captured village (as it did immediately) that the tall prisoner whom Tom Slade had brought in, was none other than the famous Major Johann Slauberstrauffn von Piffinhoeffer, excitement ran high in the neighborhood, and the towheaded young dispatch-rider from the Toul sector was hardly less of a celebrity than the terrible Prussian himself. "Paul Revere" and his compass became the subjects of much mirth, touched, as usual, with a kind of bantering evidence of genuine liking.

In face of all this, Tom bestowed all the credit on Roscoe (it would be hard to say why), and on Archibald Archer and the Big Dipper.

"Now that we've got the Big Dipper with us we ought to be able to push right through to Berlin," observed one young corporal. "They say Edison's got some new kind of a wrinkle up his sleeve, but believe me, if he's got anything to beat Paul Revere's compass, he's a winner!"

"Old Piff nearly threw a fit, I heard, when he found out that he was captured by a kid in the messenger service," another added.

"They may pull a big stroke with Mars, the god of war," still another said, "but we've got the Big Dipper on our side."

Indeed, some of them nicknamed Tom the Big Dipper, but he did not mind for, as he said soberly, he had "always liked the Big Dipper, anyway."

As the next day passed the importance of Tom's coup became known among the troops stationed in the village and was the prime topic with those who were digging the new trench line northeast of the town. Indeed, aside from the particular reasons which were presently to appear, the capture of Major von Piffinhoeffer was a "stunt" of the first order which proved particularly humiliating to German dignity. That he should have been captured at all was remarkable. That he should have been hoodwinked and brought in by a young dispatch-rider was a matter of crushing mortification to him, and must have been no less so to the German high command.

Who but Major von Piffinhoeffer had first suggested the use of the poisoned bandage in the treatment of English prisoners' wounds? Who but Major von Piffinhoeffer had devised the very scheme of contaminating streams, which Tom and Roscoe had discovered? Who but Major von Piffinhoeffer had invented the famous "circle code" which had so long puzzled and baffled Uncle Sam's Secret Service agents? Who but Major von Piffinhoeffer had first suggested putting cholera germs in rifle bullets, and tuberculosis germs in American cigarettes?

A soldier of the highest distinction was Major von Piffinhoeffer, of Heidelberg University, whose decorative junk had come direct from the grateful junkers, and whose famous eight-volume work on "Principles of Modern Torture" was a text-book in the realm. A warrior of mettle

Percy Keese Fitzhugh

was Major von Piffinhoeffer, who deserved a more glorious fate than to be captured by an American dispatch-rider!

But Tom Slade was not vain and it is doubtful if his stolid face, crowned by his shock of rebellious hair, would have shown the slightest symptom of excitement if he had captured Hindenburg, or the Kaiser himself.

In the morning he rode down to Chepoix with some dispatches and in the afternoon to St. Justen-Chaussee. He was kept busy all day. When he returned to Cantigny, a little before dark, he was told to remain at headquarters, and for a while he feared that he was going to be court-martialled for overstaying his leave.

When he was at last admitted into the presence of the commanding officer, he shifted from one foot to the other, feeling ill at ease as he always did in the presence of officialdom. The officer sat at a heavy table which had evidently been the kitchen table of the French peasant people who had originally occupied the poor cottage. Signs of petty German devastation were all about the humble, low-ceiled place, and they seemed to evidence a more loathsome brutality even than did the blighted country which Tom had ridden through.

Apparently everything which could show an arrogant contempt of the simple family life which had reigned there had been done. There was a kind of childish spitefulness in the sword thrusts through the few pictures which hung on the walls. The German genius for destruction and wanton vandalism was evident in broken knick-knacks and mottoes of hate and bloody vengeance scrawled upon floor and wall.

It did Tom's heart good to see the resolute, capable American officers sitting there attending to their business in quiet disregard of all these silly, vulgar signs of impotent hate and baffled power.

"When you first met these Germans," the officer asked, "did the big fellow have anything to say?"

"He asked us some questions," said Tom.

"Yes? Now what did he ask you?" the officer encouraged, as he reached out and took a couple of papers pinned together, which lay among others on the table.

"He seemed to be interested in transports, kind of, and the number of Americans there are here."

"Hmm. Did he mention any particular ship—do you remember?" the officer asked, glancing at the paper.

"Yes, he did. *Texas Pioneer*. I don't remember whether it was Texan or Texas."

"Oh, yes," said the officer.

"We didn't tell him anything," said Tom.

"No, of course not."

The officer sat whistling for a few seconds, and scrutinizing the papers.

"Do you remember the color of the officer's eyes?" he suddenly asked.

"It was only in the dark we saw him."

"Yes, surely. So you didn't get a very good look at him."

"I saw he had a nose shaped like a carrot, kind of," said Tom ingenuously.

Both of the officers smiled.

"I mean the big end of it," said Tom soberly.

The two men glanced at each other and laughed outright. Tom did not quite appreciate what they were laughing at but it encouraged him to greater boldness, and shifting from one foot to the other, he said,

"The thing I noticed specially was how his mouth went sideways when he talked, so one side of it seemed to slant the same as his moustache, like, and the other didn't."

The officers smiled at each other again, but the one quizzing Tom looked at him shrewdly and seemed interested.

"I mean the two ends of his moustache that stuck up like the Kaiser's—"

"Oh, yes."

"I mean they didn't slant the same when he talked. One was crooked."

Again the officers smiled and the one who had been speaking said thoughtfully,

"I see."

Tom shifted back to his other foot while the officer seemed to ruminate.

"He had a breed mark, too," Tom volunteered.

"A what?"

"Breed mark—it's different from a species mark," he added naively.

The officer looked at him rather curiously. "And what do you call a breed mark?" he asked.

Tom looked at the other man who seemed also to be watching him closely. He shifted from one foot to the other and said,

"It's a scout sign. A man named Jeb Rushmore told me about it. All trappers know about it. It was his ear, how it stuck out, like."

He shifted to the other foot.

"Yes, go on."

"Nothing, only that's what a breed sign is. If Jeb Rushmore saw a bear and afterwards way off he saw another bear he could tell if the first bear was its grandmother—most always he could.

"Hmm. I see," said the officer, plainly interested and watching Tom curiously. "And that's what a breed sign is, eh?"

"Yes, sir. Eyes ain't breed signs, but ears are. Feet are, too, and different ways of walking are, but ears are the best of all—that's one sure thing."

"And you mean that relationships can be determined by these breed signs?"

Percy Keese Fitzhugh

"I don't mean people just looking like each other," Tom explained, "'cause any way animals don't look like each other in the face. But you got to go by breed signs. Knuckles are good signs, too."

"Well, well," said the officer, "that's very fine, and news to me."

"Maybe you were never a scout," said Tom naively.

"So that if you saw your Prussian major's brother or son somewhere, where you had reason to think he would be, you'd know him—you'd recognize him?"

Tom hesitated and shifted again. It was getting pretty deep for him.

CHAPTER TWENTY

THE MAJOR'S PAPERS

It was perfectly evident that the officer's purpose in sending for Tom, whatever that was, was considerably affected by the boy's own remarks, and he now, after pondering a few moments, handed Tom the two papers which he had been holding.

"Just glance that over and then I'll talk to you," he said.

Tom felt very important, indeed, and somewhat perturbed as well, for though he had carried many dispatches it had never been his lot to know their purport.

"If you know the importance and seriousness of what I am thinking of letting you do," the officer said, "perhaps it will help you to be very careful and thorough."

"Yes, sir," said Tom, awkwardly.

"All right, just glance that over."

The two papers were clipped together, and as Tom looked at the one on top he saw that it was soiled and creased and written in German. The other was evidently a translation of it. It seemed to be a letter the first part of which was missing, and this is what Tom read:

"but, as you say, everything for the Fatherland. If you receive this let them know that I'll have my arms crossed and to be careful before they shoot. If you don't get this I'll just have to take my chance. The other way isn't worth trying. As for the code key, that will be safe enough— they'll never find it. If it wasn't for the—English service— (worn and undecipherable) —as far as that's concerned. As far as I can ascertain we'll go on the T.P. There was some inquiry about my close relationship to you, but nothing serious. All you have to do is cheer when they play the S.S.B. over here. It isn't known if Schmitter had the key to this when they caught him because he died on Ellis Island. But it's being abandoned to be on the safe side. I have notice from H. not to use it after sending this letter. If we can get the new one in your hands before— (text undecipherable)—in time so it can be used   through Mexico.

"I'll have much information to communicate verbally in T. and A. matters, but will bring nothing in—form but key and   credentials. The idea is L.'s—you remember him at Heidelberg, I dare say. I brought him back once for holiday. Met him through Handel, the fellow who was troubled with cataract. V. has furnished   funds. So don't fail to have them watch out.

"To the day,

"A. P."

"So you see some one is probably coming over on the *Texas Pioneer*," said the officer, as he took the papers from bewildered Tom, "and we'd like to get hold of that fellow.

The only trouble is we don't know who he is."

It was quite half a minute before Tom could get a grip on himself, so dark and mysterious had seemed this extraordinary communication. And it was not until afterward, when he was alone and not handicapped by his present embarrassment, that certain puzzling things about it became clear to him. At present he depended wholly upon what his superior told him and thought of nothing else.

"That was taken from your tall friend," said the officer, "and it means, if it means anything, that somebody or other closely related to him is coming over to France on the *Texas Pioneer*. From his mention of the name to you I take it that is what T. P. means.

"Now, my boy, we want to get hold of this fellow—he's a spy. Apparently, he won't have anything incriminating about him. My impression is that he's in the army and hopes to get himself captured by his friends. Yet he may desert and take a chance of getting into Germany through Holland. About the only clew there is, is the intimation that he's related to the prisoner. He may look like him. We've been trying to get in communication with Dieppe, where this transport is expected to dock to-morrow, but the wires seem to be shot into a tangle again.

"Do you think you could make Dieppe before morning— eighty to ninety miles?"

"Yes, sir. The first twenty or so will be bad on account of shell holes, I heard they threw as far as Forges."

"Hmm," said the officer, drumming with his fingers. "We'll leave all that to you. The thing is to get there before morning."

Percy Keese Fitzhugh

"I know they never let anybody ashore before daylight," said Tom, "because I worked on a transport."

"Very well. Now we'll see if the general and others here-abouts have been overrating you. You've two things to do. One is to get to Dieppe before to-morrow morning. That's imperative. The other is to assist the authorities there to identify the writer of this letter if you can. Of course, you'll not concern yourself with anything else in the letter. I let you read it partly because of your very commendable bringing in of this important captive and partly because I want you to know how serious and important are the matters involved. I was rather impressed with what you said about—er—breed marks."

"Yes, sir."

"And I believe you're thoughtful and careful. You've ridden by night a good deal, I understand."

"Yes, sir."

"So. Now you are to ride at once to Breteuil, a little east of here, where they're holding this prisoner. You'll deliver a note I shall give you to Colonel Wallace, and he'll see to it that you have a look at the man, in a sufficiently good light. Don't be afraid to observe him closely. And whatever acuteness you may have in this way, let your country have the benefit of it."

"Yes, sir."

"It may be that some striking likeness will enable you to recognize this stranger. Possibly your special knowledge will be helpful. In any case, when you reach Dieppe, present these papers, with the letter which I shall give you, to the quartermaster there, and he will turn you over to the Secret Service men. Do whatever they tell you and help them in every way you can. I shall mention that you've seen the prisoner and observed him closely. They may have means of discovery and identification which I know nothing of, but don't be afraid to offer your help. Too much won't be expected of you in that way, but it's imperative that you reach Dieppe before morning. The roads are pretty bad, I know that. Think you can do it?"

"What you got to do, you can do," said Tom simply.

It was a favorite saying of the same Jeb Rushmore, scout and woodsman, who had told Tom about breed marks, and how they differed from mere points of resemblance. And it made him think about Jeb Rushmore.

CHAPTER TWENTY-ONE

THE MIDNIGHT RIDE OF PAUL REVERE

Swiftly and silently along the dark road sped the dispatch-rider who had come out of the East, from the far-off Toul sector, *for service as required.* All the way across bleeding, devastated France he had travelled, and having paused, as it were, to help in the little job at Cantigny, he was now speeding through the darkness toward the coast with as important a message as he had ever carried.

A little while before, as time is reckoned, he had been a Boy Scout in America and had thought it was something to hike from New York to the Catskills. Since then, he had been on a torpedoed transport, had been carried in a submarine to Germany, had escaped through that war-mad land and made his way to France, whose scarred and disordered territory he had crossed almost from one end to the other, and was now headed for almost the very point where he had first landed. Yet he was only eighteen, and no one whom he met seemed to think that his experiences had been remarkable. For in a world where all are having extraordinary experiences, those of one particular person are hardly matter for comment.

At Breteuil Tom had another look at "Major Piff," who bent his terrible, scornful gaze upon him, making poor Tom feel like an insignificant worm. But the imperious Prussian's stare netted him not half so much in the matter of valuable data as Tom derived from his rather timid scrutiny. Yet he would almost have preferred to face the muzzle of a field-piece rather than wither beneath that arrogant, contemptuous glare.

It was close on to midnight when he reached Hardivillers, passing beyond the point of the Huns' farthest advance, and sped along the straight road for Marseille-en-Froissy, where he was to leave a relay packet for Paris. From there he intended to run down to Gournay and then northwest along the highway to the coast. He thought he had plenty of time.

At Gournay they told him that some American engineers were repairing the bridge at Saumont, which had been damaged by floods, but that he might gain the north road to the coast by going back as far as Songeons and following the path along the upper Therain River, which would take him to Aumale, and bring him into the Neufchatel road.

He lost perhaps two hours in doing this, partly by reason of the extra distance and partly by reason of the muddy, and in some places submerged, path along the Therain. The stream, ordinarily hardly more than a creek, was so swollen that he had to run his machine through a veritable swamp in places, and anything approaching speed was out of the question. So difficult was his progress, what with running off the flooded road and into the stream bed, and also from his wheels sticking in the mud, that he began to fear that he was losing too much time in this discouraging business.

But there was nothing to do but go forward, and he struggled on, sometimes wheeling his machine, sometimes riding it, until at last it sank almost wheel deep in muddy water and he had to lose another half hour in cleaning out his carbureter. He feared that it might give trouble even then, but the machine labored along when the mud was not too deep, and at last, after almost superhuman effort, he and *Uncle Sam* emerged, dirty and dripping, out of a region where he could almost have made as good progress with a boat, into Aumale, where he stopped long enough to clean the grit out of his engine parts.

It was now nearly four o'clock in the morning, and his instructions were to reach Dieppe not later than five. He knew, from his own experience, that transports always discharge their thronging human cargoes early in the morning, and that every minute after five o'clock would increase the likelihood of his finding the soldiers already gone ashore and separated for the journeys to their various destinations. To reach Dieppe after the departure of the soldiers was simply unthinkable to Tom. Whatever excuse there might have been to the authorities for his failure, that also he could not allow to enter his thoughts. He had been trusted to do something and he was going to do it.

Perhaps it was this dogged resolve which deterred him from doing something which he had thought of doing; that is, acquainting the authorities at Aumale with his plight and letting them wire on to Dieppe. Surely the wires between Aumale and the coast must be working, but suppose—

Suppose the Germans should demolish those wires with a random shot from some great gun such as the monster which had bombarded Paris at a distance of seventy miles. Such a random shot might demolish Tom Slade, too, but he did not think of that. What he thought of chiefly was the inglorious role he would play if, after shifting his responsibility, he should go riding into Dieppe only to find that the faithful dots and dashes had done his work for him. Then again, suppose the wires should be tapped—there were spies everywhere, he knew that.

Whatever might have been the part of wisdom and caution, he was well past Aumale before he allowed himself to realize that he was taking rather a big chance. If there were floods in one place there might be floods in another, but—

He banished the thought from his mind. Tom Slade, motorcycle dispatch-bearer, had always regarded the villages he rushed through with a kind of patronizing condescension. His business had always been between some headquarters or other and some point of destination, and between these points he had no interest. He and *Uncle Sam* had a little pride in these matters. French children with clattering wooden shoes had clustered about him when he paused, old wives had called, "*Vive l'Amerique!*" from windows and, like the post-boy of old, he had enjoyed the prestige which was his. Should he, Tom Slade, surrender or ask for help in one of these mere incidental places along his line of travel?

What you got to do, you do, he had said, and you cannot do it by going half way and then letting some one else do the rest. He had read the *Message to Garcia* (as what scout has not), and did that bully messenger—whatever his name was—turn back because the Cuban jungle was too much for him? *He delivered the message to Garcia*, that was the point. There were swamps, and dank, tangled, poisonous vines, and venomous snakes, and the sickening breath of fever. *But he delivered the message to Garcia.*

It was sixty miles, Tom knew, from Aumale to Dieppe by the road. And he must reach Dieppe not later than five o'clock. The road was a good road, if it held nothing unexpected. The map showed it to be a good road, and as far west as this there was small danger from shell holes.

Fifty miles, and one hour!

Percy Keese Fitzhugh

Swiftly along the dark road sped the dispatch-rider who had come from the far-off blue hills of Alsace across the war-scorched area of northern France into the din and fire and stenching suffocation and red-running streams of Picardy *for service as required.* Past St. Prey he rushed; past Thiueloy, and into Mortemer, and on to the hilly region where the Eualine flows between its hilly banks. He was in and out of La Tois in half a minute.

When he passed through Neufchatel several poilus, lounging at the station, hailed him cheerily in French, but he paid no heed, and they stood gaping, seeing his bent form and head thrust forward with its shock of tow hair flying all about.

Twenty miles, and half an hour!

Through St. Authon he sped, raising a cloud of dust, his keen eyes rivetted upon the road ahead, and down into the valley where a tributary of the Bethune winds its troubled way—past Le Farge, past tiny, picturesque Loix, into an area of 'lowland where an isolated cottage seemed like a lonely spectre of the night as he passed, on through Mernoy to the crossing at Chabris, and then—

CHAPTER TWENTY-TWO

"UNCLE SAM"

Tom Slade stood looking with consternation at the scene before him. His trusty motorcycle which had borne him so far stood beside him, and as he steadied it, it seemed as if this mute companion and co-patriot which he had come to love, were sharing his utter dismay. Almost at his very feet rushed a boisterous torrent, melting the packed earth of the road like wax in a tropic sunshine, and carrying its devastating work of erosion to the very spot where he stood.

In a kind of cold despair, he stooped, reached for a board which lay near, and retreating a little, stood upon it, watching the surging water in its heedless career. This one board was all that was left of the bridge over which Tom Slade and *Uncle Sam* were to have rushed in their race with the dawn. Already the first glimmering of gray was discernible in the sky behind him, and Tom looked at *Uncle Sam* as if for council in his dilemma. The dawn would not require any bridge to get across.

"We're checked in our grand drive, kind of," he said, with a pathetic disappointment which his odd way of putting it did not disguise. "We're checked, that's all, just like the Germans were—kind of."

Percy Keese Fitzhugh

He knelt and let down the rest of his machine so that it might stand unaided, as if he would be considerate of those mud-covered, weary wheels.

And meanwhile the minutes passed.

"Anyway, you did *your* part," he muttered. And then, "If you only could swim."

It was evident that the recent rains had swollen the stream which ordinarily flowed in the narrow bed between slanting shores so that the rushing water filled the whole space between the declivities and was even flooding the two ends of road which had been connected by a bridge. An old ramshackle house, which Tom thought might once have been a boathouse, stood near, the water lapping its underpinning. Close by it was a buoyed mooring float six or eight feet square, bobbing in the rushing water. One of the four air-tight barrels which supported it had caught in the mud and kept the buoyant, raft-like platform from being carried downstream in the rush of water.

Holding his flashlight to his watch Tom saw that it was nearly fifteen minutes past four and he believed that about forty miles of road lay ahead of him. Slowly, silently, the first pale tint of gray in the sky behind him took on a more substantial hue, revealing the gaunt, black outlines of trees and painting the sun-dried, ragged shingles on the little house a dull silvery color.

"Anyway, you stood by me and it ain't your fault," Tom muttered disconsolately. He turned the handle bar this way and that, so that *Uncle Sam's* one big eye peered uncannily across the flooded stream and flickered up the road upon the other side, which wound up the hillside and away into the country beyond. The big, peering eye seemed to look longingly upon that road.

Then Tom was seized with a kind of frantic rebellion against fate—the same futile passion which causes a convict to wrench madly at the bars of his cell. The glimpse of that illuminated stretch of road across the flooded stream drove him to distraction. Baffled, powerless, his wonted stolidness left him, and he cast his eyes here and there with a sort of challenge born of despair and desperation.

Slowly, gently, the hazy dawn stole over the sky and the roof of dried and ragged shingles seemed as if it were covered with gray dust. Presently the light would flicker upon those black, mad waters and laugh at Tom from the other side.

And meanwhile the minutes passed.

He believed that he could swim the torrent and make a landing even though the rush of water carried him somewhat downstream. But what about *Uncle Sam*? He turned off the searchlight and still *Uncle Sam* was clearly visible now, standing, waiting. He could count the spokes in the wheels.

The spokes in the wheels—*the spokes*. With a sudden inspiration born of despair, Tom looked at that low, shingled roof. He could see it fairly well now. The gray dawn had almost caught up with him.

And meanwhile the minutes passed!

In a frantic burst of energy he took a running jump, caught the edge of the roof and swung himself upon it. In the thin haze his form was outlined there, his shock of light hair jerking this way and that, as he tore off one shingle after another, and threw them to the ground. He was racing now, as he had not raced before, and there was upon his square,

Percy Keese Fitzhugh

homely face that look of uncompromising resolution which the soldier wears as he goes over the top with his bayonet fixed.

Leaping to the ground again he gathered up some half a dozen shingles, selecting them with as much care as his desperate haste would permit. Then he hurriedly opened the leather tool case on his machine and tumbled the contents about until he found the roll of insulated wire which he always carried.

His next work was to split one of the shingles over his knee so that he had a strip of wood about two inches wide. It took him but so many seconds to jab four or five holes through this, and adjusting it between two slopes of the power wheel so that it stood crossways and was re-enforced by the spokes themselves, he proceeded to bind it in place with the wire. Then he moved the wheel gently around, and found that the projecting edge of wooden strip knocked against the mud-guard. Hesitating not a second he pulled and bent and twisted the mud-guard, wrenching it off. The wheel revolved freely now. The spokes were beginning to shine in the brightening light.

And meanwhile the seconds passed!

It was the work of hardly a minute to bind three other narrow strips of shingle among the spokes so that they stood more or less crossways. There was no time to place and fasten more, but these, at equal intervals, forming a sort of cross within the wheel, were quite sufficient, Tom thought, for his purpose. It was necessary to shave the edges of the shingles somewhat, after they were in place, so that they would not chafe against the axle-bars. But this was also the hurried work of a few seconds, and then Tom moved his machine to the old mooring float and lifted it upon the bobbing platform.

He must work with the feverish speed of desperation for the float was held by no better anchor than one of its supporting barrels embedded in the mud. If he placed his weight or that of *Uncle Sam* upon the side of the float already in the water the weight would probably release the mud-held barrel and the float, with himself and *Uncle Sam* upon it, would be carried willy-nilly upon the impetuous waters.

And meanwhile—How plainly he could distinguish the trees now, and the pale stars stealing away into the obscurity of the brightening heavens.

With all the strength that he could muster he wrenched a board from the centre of the platform, and moving his arm about in the opening felt the rushing water beneath.

The buoyancy of the air-tight barrels, one of which was lodged under each corner of the float, was such that with Tom and his machine upon the planks the whole platform would float six or eight inches free of the water. To pole or row this unwieldy raft in such a flood would have been quite out of the question, and even in carrying out the plan which Tom now thought furnished his only hope, he knew that the sole chance of success lay in starting right. If the float, through premature or unskilful starting, should get headed downstream, there would be no hope of counteracting its impetus.

Lifting his machine, he lowered it carefully into the opening left by the torn-off plank, until the pedals rested upon the planks on either side and the power wheel was partially submerged. So far, so good.

In less than a minute now he would either succeed or fail. It was necessary first to alter the position of the float slightly so that the opening left by the plank pointed across and slightly upstream. He had often noticed how the pilot of a ferryboat directs his craft above or below the point of landing to counteract the rising or ebbing tide, and this was his intention now; but to neutralize the force of the water with another force not subject to direction or adjustment involved a rather nice calculation.

Very cautiously he waded out upon the precipitous, submerged bank and brought the float into position. This done, he acted with lightning rapidity. Leaping upon the freed float before it had time to swing around, he raised his machine, started it, and lowering the power wheel into the opening, steadied the machine as best he could. It was not possible to let it hang upon its pedals for he must hold it at a steep angle, and it required all his strength to manage its clumsy, furiously vibrating bulk.

But the effects of his makeshift paddle-wheel were pronounced and instantaneous. His own weight and that of the machine sufficiently submerged the racing power wheel so that the rough paddles plowed the water, sending the float diagonally across the flooded stream with tremendous force. He was even able, by inclining the upper end of the machine to right or left, to guide his clumsy craft, which responded to this live rudder with surprising promptness.

In the rapid crossing this rough ferryboat lost rather more than Tom had thought it would lose from the rush of water and it brought him close to the opposite shore at a point some fifty feet beyond the road, but he had been able to maintain its direction at least to the extent of heading shoreward and preventing the buoyant float from fatal swirling, which would have meant loss of control altogether.

Perhaps it was better that his point of landing was some distance below the road, where he was able to grasp at an overhanging tree with one hand while shutting his power off and holding fast to his machine with the other. A landing would have been difficult anywhere else.

Even now he was in the precarious position of sitting upon a limb in a rather complicated network of small branches and foliage, hanging onto his motorcycle for dear life, while the buoyant float went swirling and bobbing down the flood.

It had taken him perhaps five minutes to prepare for his crossing and about thirty seconds to cross. But his strategic position was far from satisfactory. And already the more substantial light of the morning revealed the gray road winding ribbon-like away into the distance, the first glints of sunlight falling upon its bordering rocks and trees as if to taunt and mock him.

And meanwhile the minutes passed.

Percy Keese Fitzhugh

CHAPTER TWENTY-THREE

UP A TREE

In military parlance, Tom had advanced only to be caught in a pocket. There he sat, astride a large limb, hanging onto the heavy machine, which depended below him just free of the water. He had, with difficulty, moved his painful grip upon a part of the machine's mechanism and succeeded in clutching the edge of the forward wheel. This did not cut his hands so much, but the weight was unbearable in his embarrassed attitude.

Indeed, it was not so much his strength, which was remarkable, that enabled him to keep his hold upon this depending dead weight, as it was sheer desperation. It seemed to be pulling his arms out of their sockets, and his shoulders ached incessantly. At the risk of losing his balance altogether he sought relief by the continual shifting of his position but he knew that the strain was too great for him and that he must let go presently.

It seemed like a mockery that he should have gained the shore only to be caught in this predicament, and to see his trusty machine go tumbling into the water beyond all hope of present recovery, simply because he could not hang on to it.

Well, then, he *would* hang on to it. He would hang on to it though every muscle of his body throbbed, though his arms were dragged out, and though he collapsed and fell from that limb himself in the last anguish of the aching strain. He and *Uncle Sam*, having failed, would go down together.

And meanwhile the minutes passed and *Uncle Sam* and Tom were reflected, inverted, in the water where the spreading light was now flickering. How strange and grotesque they looked, upside down and clinging to each other for dear life and wriggling in the ripples of rushing water. *Uncle Sam* seemed to be holding *him* up. It was all the same—they were partners.

He noticed in the water something which he had not noticed before—the reflection of a short, thick, broken branch projecting from the heavy limb he was straddling. He glanced about and found that it was behind him. His stooping attitude, necessitated by the tremendous drag on his arms, prevented him even from looking freely behind him, and in trying to do so he nearly fell. The strain he was suffering was so great that the least move caused him pain.

But by looking into the water he was able to see that this little stub of a limb might serve as a hook on which the machine might be hung if he could clear away the leafy twigs which grew from it, and if he could succeed in raising the cycle and slipping the wheel over it. That would not end his predicament but it would save the machine, relieve him for a few moments, and give him time to think.

For a few moments! They were fleeting by—the moments.

There is a strength born of desperation—a strength of will which is conjured into physical power in the last extremity. It is when the frantic, baffled spirit calls aloud to rally every

Percy Keese Fitzhugh

failing muscle and weakening nerve. It is then that the lips tighten and the eyes become as steel, as the last reserves waiting in the entrenchments of the soul are summoned up to re-enforce the losing cause.

And there in that tree, on the brink of the heedless, rushing waters which crossed the highroad to Dieppe was going to be fought out one of the most desperate battles of the whole war. There, in the mocking light of the paling dawn, Tom Slade, his big mouth set like a vice, and with every last reserve he could command, was going to make his last cast of the dice—let go, give up—or, *hold on.*

Let go! Of all the inglorious forms of defeat or surrender! *To let go!* To be struck down, to be taken prisoner, to be—

But to *let go!* The bulldog, the snapping turtle, seemed like very heroes now.

"He always said I had a good muscle—he liked to feel it," he muttered. "And besides, *she* said she guessed I was strong."

He was thinking of Margaret Ellison, away back in America, and of Roscoe Bent, as he had known him there. When he muttered again there was a beseeching pathos in his voice which would have pierced the heart of anyone who could have seen him struggling still against fate, in this all but hopeless predicament.

But no one saw him except the sun who was raising his head above the horizon as a soldier steals a cautious look over the trench parapet.

There would be no report of this affair.

He lowered his chest to the limb, wound his legs around it

and for a second lay there while he tightened and set his legs, as one will tighten a belt against some impending strain. Not another fraction of an inch could he have tightened those encircling legs.

And now the fateful second was come. It had to come quickly for his strength was ebbing. There is a pretty dependable rule that if you can just manage to lift a weight with both hands, you can just about *budge* it with one hand. Tom had tried this at Temple Camp with a visiting scout's baggage chest. With both hands he had been barely able to lift it by its strap. With one hand he had been able to *budge* it for the fraction of a second. But there had been no overmastering incentive—and no reserves called up out of the depths of his soul.

He could feel his breast palpitating against the limb, drawn tight against it by the dead weight. Yet he could not put his desperate purpose to the test.

And so a second—two, three, seconds—were wasted.

"I won't let go," he muttered through his teeth. "I wish I could wipe the sweat off my hand." Then, as if his dogged resolution were not enough, he added, almost appealingly, "Don't *you* drop and—and go back on me."

Uncle Sam only swung a little in the breeze and wriggled like an eel in the watery mirror.

Slowly Tom loosened his perspiring left hand, not daring to withdraw it. The act seemed to communicate an extra strain to every part of his body. Of all the fateful moments of his life, this seemed to be the most tense. Then, in an impulse of desperation, he drew his left hand away.

Percy Keese Fitzhugh

"I won't—let—go," he muttered.

The muscles on his taut right arm stood out like cords. His forearm throbbed with an indescribable, pulling pain. There was a feeling of dull soreness in his shoulder blade. His perspiring hand closed tighter around the wheel's rim and he could feel his pulse pounding. His fingers tingled as if they had been asleep. Then his hand slipped a little.

CHAPTER TWENTY-FOUR

"TO HIM THAT OVERCOMETH"

Whether merely from the change of an eighth of an inch or so in its hold upon the rim, or because his palm fitted better around the slight alteration of curve, Tom was conscious of the slightest measure of relief.

As quickly as he dared (for he knew that any sudden move would be fatal), he reached behind him with his left arm and, groping for the stub of limb, tore away from it the twigs which he knew would form an obstacle to placing the wheel rim with its network of spokes over this short projection.

The dead soreness of his straining shoulder blade ran down his arm, which throbbed painfully. His twitching, struggling fingers, straining against the weight which was forcing them open, clutched the rim. They were burning and yet seemed numb. Oh, if he could only wipe his palm and that rim with a dry handkerchief! He tightened his slipping fingers again and again. The muscles of his arm smarted as from a blow. He tightened his lips—and that seemed to help.

Carefully, though his aching breast pounded against the limb, he brought back his left hand, cautiously rubbed it against his khaki shirt, then encircled it about the rim. For a moment the weight seemed manageably light in the quick relief he felt.

Availing himself of the slight measure of refreshment he raised the machine a trifle, a trifle more, squirmed about to get in better position, bent, strained, got the bulky thing past his clutching legs, exerted every muscle of chest and abdomen, which now could assume some share of the strain, and by a superhuman effort of litheness and dexterity and all the overwhelming power of physical strength and frenzied resolution, he succeeded in slipping the wheel rim over the stubby projection behind him.

If he had been running for ten miles he could not have been more exhausted. His breast heaved with every spasmodic breath he drew. His shoulder blades throbbed like an aching tooth. His dripping palm was utterly numb. For a few brief, precious seconds he sat upon the limb with a sense of unutterable relief, and mopped his beaded forehead. And the sun's full, round face smiled approvingly upon him.

Meanwhile the minutes flew.

Hurrying now, he scrambled down the tree trunk where he had a better and less discouraging view of the situation. He saw that *Uncle Sam* hung about five feet from the brink and just clear of the water. If the bank on this side was less precipitous than on the other there would be some prospect of rescuing his machine without serious damage. He could afford to let it get wet provided the carburetor and magneto were not submerged and the gas tank—

The gas tank. That thought stabbed him. Could the gasoline have flowed out of the tank while the machine was hanging up and down? That would bring the supply hole, with its perforated screw-cover, underneath.

He waded cautiously into the water and found to his infinite relief that the submerged bank formed a gentle slope. He could not go far enough to lift his machine, but he could reach to wiggle it off its hook and then guide it, in some measure, enough to ease its fall and keep its damageable parts clear of the water. At least he believed he could. In any event, he had no alternative choice and time was flying. After what he had already done he felt he could do anything. Success, however wearying and exhausting, gives one a certain working capital of strength, and having succeeded so far he would not now fail. His success in crossing had given him that working capital of resolution and incentive whence came his superhuman strength and overmastering resolve in that lonely tree. And he would not fail now.

Yet he could not bring himself to look at his watch. He was willing to venture a guess, from the sun, as to what time it was, but he could not clinch the knowledge by a look at the cruel, uncompromising little glass-faced autocrat in his pocket. He preferred to work in the less disheartening element of uncertainty. He did not want to know the hard, cold truth—not till he was moving.

Here now was the need of nice calculating, and Tom eyed the shore and the tree and the machine with the appraising glance of a wrestler eyeing his opponent. He broke several branches from the tree, laying them so as to form a kind of springy, leafy mound close to the brink. Then standing knee-deep he wiggled the wheel's rim very cautiously out to the end of its hanger, so that it just balanced there.

One more grand drive, one more effort of unyielding strength and accurate dexterity and—*he would be upon the road.*

The thought acted as a stimulant. Lodging one hand under

the seat of the machine and the other upon a stout bar of the mechanism which he thought would afford him just the play and swing he needed, he joggled the wheel off its hanger, and with a wide sweep, in which he skillfully minimized the heavy weight, he swung the machine onto the springy bed which he had made to receive it.

Then, as the comrade of a wounded soldier may bend over him, he knelt down beside his companion upon the make-shift, leafy couch.

"Are you all right?" he asked in the agitation of his triumphant effort.

Uncle Sam did not answer.

He stood the machine upright and lowered the rest so that it could stand unaided; and he tore away the remnant of mud-guard which *Uncle Sam* had sacrificed in his role of combination engine and paddle-wheel.

"You've got the wires all tangled up in your spokes," Tom said; "you look like a—a wreck. What do you want with those old sticks of shingles? How are you off for gas—you—you old tramp?"

Uncle Sam did not answer.

"Anyway, you're all right," Tom panted; "only my arm is worse than your old mud-guard. We're a pair of—Can't you speak?" he added breathing the deadly fatigue he felt and putting his foot upon the pedal. "What—do—you—say? Huh?"

And then *Uncle Sam* answered.

"Tk-tk-tk-tk-tk-r-r-r-r-r-r-r—Never mind your arm. Come ahead—hurry," he seemed to say.

CHAPTER TWENTY-FIVE

"WHAT YOU HAVE TO DO—"

Swiftly along the sun-flecked road sped the dispatch-rider. In the mellow freshness of the new day he rode, and the whir of his machine in its lightning flight mingled with the cheery songs of the birds, whose early morning chorus heartened and encouraged him. There was a balm in the fragrant atmosphere of the cool, gray morning which entered the soul of Tom Slade and whispered to him, *There is no such word as fail.*

Out of the night he had come, out of travail, and brain-racking perplexity and torturing effort, crossing rushing waters and matching his splendid strength and towering will against obstacles, against fate, against everything.

As he held the handle-bar of *Uncle Sam* in that continuous handshake which they knew so well, his right arm felt numb and sore, and his whole body ached. *Uncle Sam's* big, leering glass eye was smashed, his mud-guard wrenched off, and dried mud was upon his wheels. His rider's uniform was torn and water-soaked, his face black with grime. They made a good pair.

Never a glance to right or left did the rider give, nor so much as a perfunctory nod to the few early risers who paused to stare at him as he sped by. In the little hamlet of Persan an old Frenchman sitting on a rustic seat before the village inn, removed his pipe from his mouth long enough to call,

"*La cote?*"

But never a word did the rider answer. Children, who, following the good example of the early bird, were already abroad, scurried out of his way, making a great clatter in their wooden shoes, and gaping until he passed beyond their sight.

Over the bridge at Soignois he rushed, making its ramshackle planks rattle and throw up a cloud of dust from between the vibrating seams. Out of this cloud he emerged like a gray spectre, body bent, head low, gaze fixed and intense, leaving a pandemonium of dust and subsiding echoes behind him.

At Virneu an old housewife threw open her blinds and seeing the dusty khaki of the rider, summoned her brood, who waved the tricolor from the casement, laughing and calling, "*Vive l'Amerique!*"

Their cheery voices and fraternal patriotism did cause Tom to turn his head and call,

"*Merci. Vive la France!*"

And they answered again with a torrent of French.

The morning was well established as he passed through Chuisson, and a clock upon a romantic, medieval-looking little tower told him that it lacked but ten minutes of five o'clock.

A feeling of doubt, almost of despair, seized upon him and he called in that impatient surliness which springs from tense anxiety, asking an old man how far it was to Dieppe.

The man shrugged his shoulders and shook his head in polite confession that he did not understand English.

In his anxiety it irritated Tom. "What *do* you know?" he muttered.

Out of Chuisson he labored up a long hill, and though *Uncle Sam* made no more concession to it than to slacken his unprecedented rate of speed the merest trifle, the difference communicated itself to Tom at once and it seemed, by contrast, as if they were creeping. On and up *Uncle Sam* went, plying his way sturdily, making a great noise and a terrific odor—dogged, determined and irresistible.

But the rider stirred impatiently. Would they ever, *ever*, reach the top? And when they should, there would be another hamlet in a valley, another bridge, more stupid people who could not speak English, more villages, more bends in the road, still other villages, and then—another hill.

It seemed to Tom that he had been travelling for ten years and that there was to be no end of it. Ride, ride, ride—it brought him nowhere. His right arm which had borne that tremendous strain, was throbbing so that he let go the handle-bar from time to time in the hope of relief. It was the pain of acute tiredness, for which there could be no relief but rest. Just to throw himself down and rest! Oh, if he could only lay that weary, aching arm across some soft pillow and leave it there—just leave it there. Let it hang, bend it, hold it above him, lay it on *Uncle Sam's* staunch, unfeeling arm of steel, he could not, *could* not, get it rested.

The palm of his hand tingled with a kind of irritating feeling like chilblains, and he must be continually removing one or other hand from the bar so that he could reach one with the other. It did not help him keep his poise. If he could only scratch his right hand once and be done with it! But it annoyed him like a fly.

Up, up, up, they went, and passed a quaint, old, thatch-roofed house. Crazy place to build a house! And the people in it—probably all they could do was to shrug their shoulders in that stupid way when asked a question in English.

He was losing his morale—was this dispatch-rider.

But near the top of the hill he regained it somewhat. Perhaps he could make up for this lost time in some straight, level reach of road beyond.

Up, up, up, plowed *Uncle Sam*, one lonely splinter of shingle still bound within his spokes, and his poor, dented headlight bereft of its dignity.

"I've an idea the road turns north about a mile down," Tom said to himself, "and runs around through—"

The words stopped upon his lips as *Uncle Sam*, still laboring upward, reached level ground, and as if to answer Tom out of his own uncomplaining and stouter courage, showed him a sight which sent his faltering hope skyward and started his heart bounding.

For there below them lay the vast and endless background of the sea, throwing every intervening detail of the landscape into insignificance. There it was, steel blue in the brightening sunlight and glimmering here and there in changing white, where perhaps some treacherous rock or bar lay just

Percy Keese Fitzhugh

submerged. And upon it, looking infinitesimal in the limitless expanse, was something solid with a column of black smoke rising and winding away from it and dissolving in the clear, morning air.

"There you are!" said Tom, patting *Uncle Sam* patronizingly in a swift change of mood. "See there? That's the Atlantic Ocean—that is. *Now* will you hurry? That's a ship coming in —see? I bet it's a whopper, too. Do you know what—what's off beyond there?" he fairly panted in his excitement; "do you? You old French hobo, you? *America!* That's where *I* came from. *Now* will you hurry? That's Dieppe, where the white[2] is and those steeples, see? And way across there on the other side is America!"

For *Uncle Sam*, notwithstanding his name, was a French motorcycle and had never seen America.

[2] Dieppe's famous beach.

CHAPTER TWENTY-SIX

A SURPRISE

Down the hill coasted *Uncle Sam*, bearing his rider furiously onward. A fence along the wayside seemed like a very entanglement of stakes and pickets. Then it was gone. A house loomed up in view, grew larger, and was gone. A cow that was grazing in a field languidly raised her head, blinked her eyes, and stood as if uncertain whether she had really seen something pass or not.

They were in the valley now and the sea was no longer discernible. On they rushed with a fine disdain for poor little Charos, whose village steeple appeared and disappeared like a flash of lightning. The road was broad and level and *Uncle Sam* sped along amid a cloud of dust, the bordering trees and houses flying away behind like dried leaves in a hurricane. The rider's hair was fluttering like a victorious emblem, his eyes fixed with a wild intensity.

"We'd get arrested for this in America," he muttered; "we—we should worry."

It was little *Uncle Sam* cared for the traffic laws of America.

Around the outskirts of Teurley they swept and into the

Percy Keese Fitzhugh

broad highway like a pair of demons, and a muleteer, seeing discretion to be the better part of valor, drove his team well to the side—far enough, even, to escape any devilish contamination which this unearthly apparition might diffuse.

They had reached a broad highway, one of those noble roads which Napoleon had made. They could not go wrong now. They passed a luxurious chateau, then a great hotel where people haled them in French. Then they passed an army auto truck loaded with mattresses, with the bully old initials U. S. A. on its side. Two boys in khaki were on the seat.

"Is the *Texas Pioneer* in?" Tom yelled.

"What?" one of them called back.

"He's deaf or something," muttered Tom; "we—should worry."

On they sped till the road merged into a street lined with shops, where children in wooden shoes and men in blouses shuffled about. Tom thought he had never seen people so slow in his life.

Now, indeed, he must make some concession to the throngs moving back and forth, and he slackened his speed, but only slightly.

"Dieppe?" he called.

"Dieppe," came the laughing answer from a passer-by, who was evidently amused at Tom's pronunciation.

"Where's the wharves?"

Again that polite shrug of the shoulders.

He took a chance with another passer-by, who nodded and pointed down a narrow street with dull brown houses tumbling all over each other, as it seemed to Tom. It was the familiar, old-world architecture of the French coast towns, which he had seen in Brest and St. Nazaire, as if all the houses had become suddenly frightened and huddled together like panicky sheep.

More leisurely now, but quickly still, rode the dispatch-rider through this narrow, surging way which had all the earmarks of the shore—damp-smelling barrels, brass lanterns, dilapidated ships' figureheads, cosy but uncleanly drinking places, and sailors.

And of all the sights save one which Tom Slade ever beheld, the one which most gladdened his heart was a neat new sign outside a stone building,

Office of United States Quartermaster.

Several American army wagons were backed up against the building and half a dozen khaki-clad boys lounged about. There was much coming and going, but it is a part of the dispatch-rider's prestige to have immediate admittance anywhere, and Tom stopped before this building and was immediately surrounded by a flattering representation of military and civilian life, both French and American.

To these he paid not the slightest heed, but carefully lowered *Uncle Sam's* rest so that his weary companion might stand alone.

"You old tramp," he said in an undertone; "stay here and take it easy. Keep away," he added curtly to a curious private who was venturing a too close inspection of *Uncle Sam's* honorable wounds.

Percy Keese Fitzhugh

"What's the matter—run into something?" he asked.

"No, I didn't," said Tom, starting toward the building.

Suddenly he stopped short, staring.

A man in civilian clothes sat tilted back in one of several chairs beside the door. He wore a little black moustache and because his head was pressed against the brick wall behind him, his hat was pushed forward giving him a rakish look which was rather heightened by an unlighted cigar sticking up out of the corner of his mouth like a piece of field artillery.

He might have been a travelling salesman waiting for his samples on the veranda of a country hotel and he had about him a kind of sophisticated look as if he took a sort of blase pleasure in watching the world go round. His feet rested upon the rung of his tilted chair, forming his knees into a sort of desk upon which lay a French newspaper. The tilting of his knees, the tilting of his chair, the tilting of his hat and the rakish tilt of his cigar, gave him the appearance of great self-sufficiency, as if, away down in his soul, he knew what he was there for, and cared not a whit whether anyone else did or not.

Tom Slade paused on the lower step and stared. Then with a slowly dawning smile supplanting his look of astonishment, he ejaculated,

"M-i-s-t-e-r *C-o-n-n-e*!"

The man made not the slightest change in his attitude except to smile the while he worked his cigar over to the other corner of his mouth. Then he cocked his head slightly sideways.

"H'lo, Tommy," said he.

CHAPTER TWENTY-SEVEN

SMOKE AND FIRE

Mr. Carleton Conne, of the United States Secret Service, had come over from Liverpool *via* Dover on a blind quest after an elusive spy. There had been a sort of undercurrent of rumor, with many extravagant trappings, that a mysterious agent of the Kaiser was on his way to Europe with secrets of a most important character. Some stories had it that he was intimately related to Bloody Bill himself; others that he gloried in a kinship with Ludendorf, while still other versions represented him as holding Mexico in the palm of his hand. Dark stories floated about and no one knew just where they originated.

One sprightly form this story took, which had been whispered in New York and then in Liverpool, was that a certain young lady (identity unknown) had talked with a soldier (identity unknown) in the Grand Central Station in New York, and that the soldier had told her that at his cantonment (cantonment not identified) there was a man in a special branch of the service (branch not mentioned) who was a cousin or a brother or a nephew or a son or something or other to a German general or statesman or something or other, and that he had got into the American army by a pretty narrow squeak. There seemed to be a unanimity of opinion in

Percy Keese Fitzhugh

the lower strata of Uncle Sam's official family in Liverpool that the soldier who had talked with the young lady was coming over on the transport *Manchester* and it was assumed (no one seemed to know exactly why) that the mysterious and sinister personage would be upon the same ship.

But no soldier had been found upon the *Manchester* who showed by his appearance that he had chatted with a young lady. Perhaps several of them had done that. It is a way soldiers have.

As for the arch spy or propagandist, he did not come forward and introduce himself as such, and though a few selected suspects of German antecedents were searched and cate-chised by Mr. Conne and others, no one was held.

And there you are.

Rumors of this kind are always in circulation and the Secret Service people run them down as a matter of precaution. But though you can run a rumor down and stab it through and through you cannot kill it. It now appeared that this German agent had sailed from Mexico and would land at Brest—with a message to some French statesman. Also it appeared that he had stolen a secret from Edison and would land at Dieppe. It had also been reported that someone had attempted to blow up the loaded transport *Texas Pioneer* on her way over.

And so Mr. Carleton Conne, of the American Secret Service, quiet, observant, uncommunicative, never too sanguine and never too skeptical, had strolled on to the *Channel Queen*, lighted his cigar, and was now tilted back in his chair outside the Quartermaster's office in Dieppe, not at all excited and waiting for the *Texas Pioneer* to dock.

He had done this because he believed that where there is a

great deal of smoke there is apt to be a little fire. He was never ruffled, never disappointed.

Tom's acquaintance with Mr. Conne had begun on the transport on which he had worked as a steward's boy, and where his observant qualities and stolid soberness had attracted and amused the detective.

"I never thought I'd see you here," said Tom, his face lighting up to an unusual degree. "I'm a dispatch-rider now. I just rode from Cantigny. I got a letter for the Quartermaster, but anyway he's got to turn me over to the Secret Service (Mr. Conne regarded him with whimsical attention as he stumbled on), because there's a plot and somebody—a spy—kind of—"

"A spy, kind of, eh?"

"And I hope the *Texas Pioneer* didn't land yet, that's one sure thing."

"It's one sure thing that she'll dock in about fifteen minutes, Tommy," said Mr. Conne rising. "Come inside and deliver your message. What's the matter with your machine? Been trying to wipe out the Germans alone and unaided, like the hero in a story book?"

Tom followed him in, clumsily telling the story of his exciting journey; "talking in chunks," as he usually did and leaving many gaps to be filled in by the listener.

"I'm glad I found you here, anyway," he finished, as if that were the only part that really counted; "'cause now I feel as if I can tell about an idea I've got. I'd of been scared to tell it to anybody else. I ain't exactly got it yet," he added, "but maybe I can help even better than they thought, 'cause as I was ridin' along I had a kind of an idea—"

"Yes?"

"Kind of. Did you ever notice how you get fool ideas when there's a steady noise going on?"

"So?" said Mr. Conne, as he led the way along a hall.

"It was the noise of my machine."

"How about the smell, Tommy?" Mr. Conne asked, glancing around with that pleasant, funny look which Tom had known so well.

"You don't get ideas from smells," he answered soberly.

In the Quartermaster's office he waited on a bench while Mr. Conne and several other men, two in uniform and two that he thought might be Secret Service men, talked in undertones. If he had been a hero in a book, to use Mr. Conne's phrase, these officials would doubtless have been assembled about him listening to his tale, but as it was he was left quite out of the conference until, near its end, he was summoned to tell of his capture of Major von Piffinhoeffer and asked if he thought he could identify a close relation of that high and mighty personage simply by seeing him pass as a total stranger.

Tom thought he might "by a special way," and explained his knowledge of breed marks and specie marks. He added, in his stolid way, that he had another idea, too. But they did not ask him what that was. One of the party, a naval officer, expressed surprise that he had ridden all the way from Cantigny and asked him if it were not true that part of the road was made impassible by floods. Tom answered that there were floods but that they were not impassible "if you knew how." The officer said he supposed Tom knew how, and Tom regarded this as a compliment.

Soon, to his relief, Mr. Conne took all the papers in the case and left the room, beckoning Tom to follow him. Another man in civilian clothes hurried away and Tom thought he might be going to the dock. It seemed to him that his rather doubtful ability to find a needle in a haystack had not made much of an impression upon these officials, and he wondered ruefully what Mr. Conne thought. He saw that his arrival with the papers had produced an enlivening effect among the officials, but it seemed that he himself was not taken very seriously. Well, in any event, he had made the trip, he had beaten the ship, delivered the message to Garcia.

"I got to go down and turn my grease cup before I forget it," he said, as they came out on the little stone portico again.

Several soldiers who were soon to see more harrowing sights than a bunged-up motorcycle, were gathered about *Uncle Sam*, gaping at him and commenting upon his disfigurements. Big U. S. A. auto trucks were passing by. A squad of German prisoners, of lowering and sullen aspect, marched by with wheelbarrows full of gray blankets. They were keeping perfect step, through sheer force of habit. Another dispatch-rider (a "local") passed by, casting a curious eye at *Uncle Sam*. A French child who sat upon the step had one of his wooden shoes full of smoky, used bullets, which he seemed greatly to prize. Several "flivver" ambulances stood across the way, new and roughly made, destined for the front. American naval and military officers were all about.

"We haven't got much time to spare, Tommy," said Mr. Conne, resuming his former seat and glancing at his watch.

"It's only a second. I just got to turn the grease cup."

He hurried down past the child, who called him "M'sieu Yankee," and elbowed his way through the group of soldiers who were standing about *Uncle Sam*.

"Your timer bar's bent," one of them volunteered.

Tom did not answer, but knelt and turned the grease cup, then wiped the nickel surfaces, bent and dented though they were, with a piece of cotton waste. Then he felt of his tires. Then he adjusted the position of the handle-bar more to his liking and as he did so the poor, dented, glassless searchlight bobbed over sideways as if to look at the middle of the street. Tom said something which was not audible to the curious onlookers. Perhaps *Uncle Sam* heard.

The local rider came jogging around the corner on his way back. His machine was American-made and a medley of nickel and polished brass. As he made the turn his polished searchlight, with a tiny flag perched jauntily upon it, seemed to be looking straight at *Uncle Sam*. And *Uncle Sam's* green-besprinkled,[3] glassless eye seemed to be leering with a kind of sophisticated look at the passing machine. It was the kind of look which the Chicago Limited might give to the five-thirty suburban starting with its load of New York commuters for East Orange, New Jersey.

[3] The effect of water on brass is to produce a greenish, superficial erosion.

CHAPTER TWENTY-EIGHT

"MADE IN GERMANY"

"Now, Tommy, let's hear your idea," said Mr. Conne, indulgently, as he worked his cigar from one corner of his mouth to the other. "I find there's generally a little fire where there's a good deal of smoke. There's somebody or other, as you say, but the trouble is we don't know who he is. We think maybe he looks like someone you've seen. We think he may have a patent ear." He looked at Tom sideways and Tom could not help laughing. Then he looked at the mysterious letter with a funny, ruminating look.

"What can we—you—do?" Tom ventured to ask, feeling somewhat squelched.

Mr. Conne screwed up his mouth with a dubious look. "Search everybody on board, two or three thousand, quiz a few, that's about all. It'll take a long time and probably reveal nothing. Family resemblances are all right when you know both members, Tommy, but out in the big world—Well, let's look this over again," he added, taking up the letter.

Tom knew that he was not being consulted. He had a feeling that his suggestion about breed marks and personal resemblances was not being taken seriously. He was glad that he

Percy Keese Fitzhugh

had not put his foot too far in by telling of his other precious idea. But he was proud of Mr. Conne's companionable attitude toward him. He was proud to be the friend of such a man. He was delighted at the thought of participation in this matter. He knew Mr. Conne liked him and had at least a good enough opinion of him to adopt the appearance of conferring with him. Mr. Conne's rather whimsical attitude toward this conference did not lessen his pride.

"Let's see now," said the detective. "This thing evidently went through Holland in code. It's a rendering."

It was easy for Tom to believe that Mr. Conne was re-reading the letter just to himself—or to himself and Tom.

"Let's see now—*but, as you say, everything for the Fatherland. If you receive this, let them know that I'll have my arms crossed and to be careful before they shoot.* I wish he'd cross his arms when he comes ashore. He's evidently planning to get himself captured. *If you don't get this I'll just have to take my chance. The other way isn't worth trying.* Hmm! Probably thought of deserting at the wharf and getting into Holland or Belgium. No, that wouldn't be worth trying. *As for the code key, that'll be safe enough—they'll never find it.* Hmm! *If it wasn't for the—*what's all this—*the English swine.* Humph! They fight pretty good for swine, don't they, Tommy? *As far as I can ascertain, we'll go on the T. P.* We know that much, anyway, thanks to you, Tommy." (Tom felt highly elated.) "*There was some inquiry about my close relationship to you, but nothing serious. All you have to do is to cheer when they play the S. S. B. over here.* Humph! That's worth knowing. *It isn't known if Schmitter had the key to this when they caught him—*

"He didn't," said Mr. Conne dryly; "I was the one who caught him.—*because he died on Ellis Island. But it's being abandoned to be on the safe side.* Safety first, hey? *I have notice from H. not to use it after sending this letter. If we can get the new one in your hands before*—Seems to be blotted out—*in time so it can be used through Mexico. I'll have much information to communicate verbally in T. and A. matters, but will bring nothing in—form but key and credentials.* He means actual, concealed or disguised form, I s'pose. *The idea is L.'s.* I suppose he means the manner of concealing the key and credentials."

"Yes," said Tom rather excitedly.

Mr. Conne glanced at him, joggled his cigar, and went on,

"*You remember him at Heidelberg, I dare say. I brought him back once for holiday. Met him through Handel, who was troubled with cataract. V. has furnished funds. So don't fall to have them watch out.*"

"Hmm!" concluded Mr. Conne ruminatively. "You see what they're up to. We caught Schmitter in Philadelphia. They think maybe Schmitter had the key of a code with him. So they're changing the code and sending the key to it across with this somebody or other. That's about the size of it. He's got a lot of information, too, in his head, where we can't get at it."

"But his credentials will have to be something that can be seen, won't they?" Tom ventured to ask.

"Prob'ly. You see, he means to desert or get captured. It's a long way round, but about the best one—for him. Think of that snake wearing Uncle Sam's uniform!"

"It makes me mad, too—kind of," said Tom.

"So he's probably got some secret means of identification about him, and probably the new code key in actual form— somewhere else than just in his head. Then there'd be a chance of getting it across even if he fell. We'll give him an acid bath and look in his shoes if we can find him. The whole thing hangs on a pretty thin thread. They used to have invisible writing on their backs till we started the acid bath."

He whistled reflectively for a few moments, while Tom struggled to muster the courage to say something that he wished to say.

"Could I tell you about that other idea of mine?" he blurted finally.

"You sure can, Tommy. That's about all we're likely to get— ideas." And he glanced at Tom again with that funny, side- ways look. "Shoot, my boy."

"It's only this," said Tom, still not without some trepidation, "and maybe you'll say it's no good. You told me once not to be thinking of things that's none of my business."

"Uncle Sam's business is our business now, Tommy boy."

"Well, then, it's just this, and I was thinking about it while I was riding just after I started away from Cantigny. Mostly I was thinking about it after I took that last special look at old Piff—"

Mr. Conne chuckled. "I see," he said encouragingly.

"Whoever that feller is," said Tom, "there's one thing sure. If he's comin' as a soldier he won't get to the front very soon, 'cause they're mostly the drafted fellers that are comin' now and they have to go in training over here. I know, 'cause I've seen lots of 'em in billets."

"Hmm," said Mr. Conne.

"So if the feller expects to go to the front and get captured pretty soon, prob'ly he's in a special unit. Maybe I might be all wrong about it—some fellers used to call me Bullhead," he added by way of shaving his boldness down a little.

But Mr. Conne, with hat tilted far down over his forehead and cigar at an outrageously rakish angle, was looking straight ahead of him, at a French flag across the way.

"Go on," he said crisply.

"Anyway, I'm sure the feller wouldn't be an engineer, 'cause mostly they're behind the lines. So I thought maybe he'd be a surgeon—"

Mr. Conne was whistling, almost inaudibly, his eyes fixed upon the flagpole opposite. "He was educated at Heidelberg," said he.

"I didn't think of that," said Tom.

"It's where he met L."

Tom said nothing. His line of reasoning seemed to be lifted quietly away from him. Mr. Conne was turning the kaleidoscope and showing him new designs. "He took L. home for the holidays," he quietly observed. "Old Piff and the boys."

"I—I didn't think of that," said Tom, rather crestfallen.

"You didn't ride fast enough and make enough noise," Mr. Conne said. His eyes were still fixed on the fluttering tricolor

Percy Keese Fitzhugh

and he whistled very low. Then he rubbed his lip with his tongue and aimed his cigar in another direction.

"They were studying medicine there, I guess," he mused.

"That's just what my idea's about," said Tom. "It ain't an idea exactly, either," he added, "but it's kind of come to me sudden-like. You know what a *hunch* is, don't you? There's something there about somebody having a cataract, and that's something the matter with your eyes; Mr. Temple had one. So maybe that feller L. that he met again is an eye doctor. Long before the war started they told Mr. Temple maybe he ought to go to Berlin to see the eye specialists there—'cause they're so fine. So maybe the spy is a surgeon and L. is an eye doctor. It says how he met him again on account of somebody having a cataract. And he said the way of bringing the code key was L.'s idea. I read about a dentist that had a piece of paper with writing on it rolled up in his tooth. He was a spy. So that made me think maybe L.'s idea had something to do with eyes or glasses, as you might say."

"Hmm! Go on. Anything else?"

"But, anyway, that ain't the idea I had. In Temple Camp there was a scout that had a little pocket looking-glass and you couldn't see anything on it but your own reflection. But all you had to do was to breathe on it and there was a picture—all mountains and a castle, like. Then it would fade away again right away. Roy Blakeley wanted to swap his scout knife for it, but the feller wouldn't do it. On the back of it it said *Made in Germany*. It just came to me sudden-like that maybe that was L.'s idea and they'd have it on a pair of spectacles. Maybe it's a kind of crazy idea, but—"

He looked doubtfully at Mr. Conne, who still sat tilted back, hat almost hiding his face, cigar sticking out from under it like a camouflaged field-piece. He was whistling very quietly, "*Oh, boy, where do we go from here?*" He had whistled that same tune more than a year before when he was waiting for a glimpse of "Dr. Curry," spy and bomb plotter, aboard the vessel on which Tom was working at that time. He had whistled it as he escorted the "doctor" down the companionway. How well Tom remembered!

"Come on, Tommy," he said, jumping suddenly to his feet.

Tom followed. But Mr. Conne did not speak; he was still busy with the tune. Only now he was singing the words. There was something portentous in the careless way he sang them. It took Tom back to the days when it was the battle hymn of the transport:

"And when we meet a pretty girl, we whisper in her ear, Oh, Boy! Oh, Joy! Where do we go from here?"

CHAPTER TWENTY-NINE

"NOW YOU SEE IT, NOW YOU DON'T"

The big transport *Texas Pioneer* came slowly about in obedience to her straining ropes and rubbed her mammoth side against the long wharf. Up and down, this way and that, slanting-wise and curved, drab and gray and white and red, the grotesque design upon her towering freeboard shone like a distorted rainbow in the sunlight. Out of the night she had come, stealing silently through the haunts where murder lurks, and the same dancing rays which had run ahead of the dispatch-rider and turned to mock him, had gilded her mighty prow as if to say, "Behold, I have reached you first."

At her rail crowded hundreds of boys in khaki, demanding in English and atrocious French to know where they were.

"Are we in France?" one called.

"Where's the Boiderberlong, anyway?" another shouted, the famous Parisian boulevard evidently being his only means of identifying France.

"Is that Napoleon's tomb?" another demanded, pointing to a little round building.

"Look at the pile of hams," shouted another gazing over the rail at a stack of that delectable. "Maybe we're in *Hamburg*!"

"This is Dippy," his neighbor corrected him.

"You mean Deppy," another said.

And so on and so on. There seemed to be hundreds of them, thousands of them, and all on a gigantic picnic.

"Which is the quickest way to Berlin?" one called, addressing the throng impartially.

"Second turn to your left."

Some of these boys would settle down in France and make it their long, final home, under little wooden crosses. But they did not seem to think of that.

At the foot of the gangplank stood the dispatch-rider and the man with the cigar. Several other men, evidently of their party, stood near by. Mr. Conne's head was cocked sideways and he scanned the gangway with a leisurely, self-assured look. Tom was shaking all over—the victim of suppressed excitement. He had been less excited on that memorable morning when he had "done his bit" at Cantigny.

It seemed to be in the air that something unusual was likely to happen. Workers, passing with their wheelbarrows and hand trucks, slackened their pace and dallied as long as they dared, near the gangplank. They were quickly moved along. Tom shifted from one foot to the other, waiting. Mr. Conne worked his cigar over to the opposite corner of his mouth and observed to an American officer that the day was going to be warm. Then he glanced up and smiled pleasantly at the boys crowding at the rail. He might have been waiting on a street corner for a car.

"Not nervous, are you?" he smiled at Tom.

"Not exactly," said Tom, with his usual candor; "but it seems as if nothing can happen at all, now that we're here. It seems different, thinking up things when you're riding along the road—kind of."

"Uh huh."

Presently the soldiers began coming down the gangplank.

"You watch for resemblances and I'll do the rest," said Mr. Conne in a low tone. "Give yourself the benefit of every doubt. Know what I mean?"

"Yes—I do."

"I can't help you there."

Tom felt a certain compunction at scrutinizing these fine, American fellows as they came down with their kits—hearty, boisterous, open-hearted. He felt that it was unworthy of him to suspect any of this laughing, bantering army, of crime— and such a crime! Treason! In the hope of catching one he must scrutinize them all, and in his generous heart it seemed to put a stigma on them all. He hoped he wouldn't see anyone who looked like Major von Piffinhoeffer. Then he hoped he would. Then he wondered if he would dare to look at him after—And suppose he should be mistaken. He did not like this sort of work at all now that he was face to face with it. He would rather be off with *Uncle Sam*, riding along the French roads, with the French children calling to him. For the first time in his life he was nervous and afraid—not of being caught but of catching someone; of the danger of suspecting and being mistaken.

Mr. Conne, who never missed anything, noticed his pertur-
bation and patted him on the shoulder saying,

"All kinds of work have to be done, Tommy."

Tom tried to smile back at him.

Down the long gangplank they came, one after another,
pushing each other, tripping each other—joking, laughing.
Among them came a young private, wearing glasses, who
was singing,

"Good-bye, Broadway. Hello, France!"

He was startled out of his careless merriment by a tap on the
shoulder from Mr. Conne, and almost before Tom realized
what had happened, he was standing blinking at one of the
other Secret Service men who was handing him back his
glasses.

"All right, my boy," said Mr. Conne pleasantly, which
seemed to wipe out any indignity the young man might have
felt.

Tom looked up the gangplank as they surged down, holding
the rail to steady them on the steep incline. Nobody seemed
to have noticed what had happened.

"Keep your mind on *your* part, Tommy," said Mr. Conne
warningly.

Tom saw that of all those in sight only one wore glasses—a
black-haired youth who kept his hands on the shoulders of
the man before him. Tom made up his mind that he, in any

Percy Keese Fitzhugh

event, would not detain this fellow on the ground of anything in his appearance, nor any of the others now in sight. He was drawn aside by Mr. Conne, however, and became the object of attention of the other Secret Service men.

Tom kept his eyes riveted upon the gangplank. One, two, more, wearing glasses, came in view, were stopped, examined, and passed on. After that perhaps a hundred passed down and away, none of them with glasses, and all of them he scrutinized carefully. Now another, with neatly adjusted rimless glasses, came down. He had a clean-cut, professional look. Tom did not take his eyes off the descending column for a second, but he heard Mr. Conne say pleasantly,

"Just a minute."

He was glad when he was conscious of this fine-looking young American passing on.

So it went.

There were some whom poor Tom might have been inclined to stop by way of precaution for no better reason than that they had a rough-and-ready look—hard fellows. He was glad—*half* glad—when Mr. Conne, for reasons of his own, detained one, then another, of these, though they wore no glasses. And he felt like apologizing to them for his momentary suspicion, as he saw them pause surprised, answer frankly and honestly and pass on.

Then came a young officer, immaculately attired, his leather leggings shining, his uniform fitting him as if he had been moulded into it. He wore little rimless eye-glasses. He might lead a raiding party for all that; but he was a bit pompous and very self-conscious. Tom was rather gratified to see him hailed aside.

Nothing.

Down they came, holding both rails and lifting their feet to swing, like school boys—hundreds of them, thousands of them, it seemed. Tom watched them all keenly as they passed out like an endless ribbon from a magician's hat. There seemed to be no end of them.

There came now a fellow whom he watched closely. He had blond hair and blue eyes, but no glasses. He looked something like—something like—oh, who? Fritzie Schmitt, whom he used to know in Bridgeboro. No, he didn't—not so much.

But his blond hair and blue eyes did not escape Mr. Conne.

Nothing.

"Watching, Tommy?"

"Yes, sir."

A hundred more, two hundred, and then a young sergeant with glasses.

While this young man was undergoing his ordeal (whatever it was, for Tom kept his eyes riveted on the gangway), there appeared the tall figure of a lieutenant. Tom thought he was of the medical corps, but he was not certain. He seemed to be looking down at Mr. Conne's little group, with a fierce, piercing stare. He wore horned spectacles of goodly circumference and as Tom's eyes followed the thick, left wing of these, he saw that it embraced an ear which stood out prominently. Both the ear and the piercing eagle gaze set him

Percy Keese Fitzhugh

all agog.

Should he speak? The lieutenant was gazing steadfastly down at Mr. Conne and coming nearer with every step. Of course, Mr. Conne would stop him anyway, but—To mention that piercing stare and that ear after the man had been stopped for the more tangible reason—there would be no triumph in that.

Tom's hand trembled like a leaf and his voice was unsteady as he turned to Mr. Conne, and said.

"This one coming down—the one that's looking at you—he looks like—and I notice—"

"Put your hands down, my man," called Mr. Conne peremptorily, at the same time leaping with the agility of a panther up past the descending throng. "I'll take those."

But Tom Slade had spoken first. He did not know whether Mr. Conne's sudden dash had been prompted by his words or not. He saw him lift the heavy spectacles off the man's ears and with beating heart watched him as he came down alongside the lieutenant.

"Going to throw them away, eh?" he heard Mr. Conne say.

Evidently the man, seeing another's glasses examined, had tried to remove his own before he reached the place of inspection. Mr. Conne, who saw everything, had seen this. But Tom had spoken before Mr. Conne moved and he was satisfied.

"All right, Tommy," said Mr. Conne in his easy way. "You beat me to it."

Tom hardly knew what took place in the next few moments. He saw Mr. Conne breathe upon the glasses, was conscious of soldiers slackening their pace to see and hear what was going on, and of their being ordered forward. He saw the two men who were with Mr. Conne standing beside the tall lieutenant, who seemed bewildered. He noticed (it is funny how one notices these little things amid such great things) the little ring of red upon the lieutenant's nose where the glasses had sat.

"There you are, see?" he heard Mr. Conne say quietly, breathing heavily upon the glasses and holding them up to the light, for the benefit of his colleagues. "B L—two dots—X—see—Plain as day. See there, Tommy!"

He breathed upon them again and held them quickly up so that Tom could see.

"Yes, sir," Tom stammered, somewhat perturbed at such official attention.

"Look in the other one, too, Tommy—now—quick!"

"Oh, yes," said Tom as the strange figures die away. He felt very proud, and not a little uncomfortable at being drawn into the centre of things. And he did not feel slighted as he saw Mr. Conne and the captive lieutenant, and the other officials whom he did not know, start away thoughtless of anything else in the stress of the extraordinary affair. He followed because he did not know what else to do, and he supposed they wished him to follow. Outside the wharf he got *Uncle Sam* and wheeled him along at a respectful distance behind these high officials. So he had one companion. Several times Mr. Conne looked back at him and smiled. And once he said in that funny way of his,

Percy Keese Fitzhugh

"All right, Tommy?"

"Yes, sir," Tom answered, trudging along. He had been greatly agitated, but his wonted stolidness was returning now. Probably he felt more comfortable and at home coming along behind with *Uncle Sam* than he would have felt in the midst of this group where the vilest treason walked baffled, but unashamed, in the uniform of Uncle Sam.

Once Mr. Conne turned to see if Tom were following. His cigar was stuck up in the corner; of his mouth as usual and he gave Tom a whimsical look.

"You hit the Piff family at both ends, didn't you, Tommy."

"Y-yes, sir," said Tom.

CHAPTER THIRTY

HE DISAPPEARS

Swiftly and silently along the quiet, winding road sped the dispatch-rider. Away from the ocean he was hurrying, where the great ships were coming in, each a fulfilment and a challenge; away from scenes of debarkation where Uncle Sam was pouring his endless wealth of courage and determination into bleeding, suffering, gallant France.

Past the big hotel he went, past the pleasant villa, through village and hamlet, and farther and farther into the East, bound for the little corner of the big salient whence he had come.

He bore with him a packet and some letters. One was to be left at Neufchatel; others at Breteuil. There was one in particular for Cantigny. His name was mentioned in it, but he did not know that. He never concerned himself with the contents of his papers.

So he sped along, thinking how he would get a new head-light for *Uncle Sam* and a new mud-guard. He thought the people back at Cantigny would wonder what had happened to his machine. He had no thought of telling them. There was nothing to tell.

Percy Keese Fitzhugh

Swiftly and silently along the road he sped, the dispatch-rider who had come from the blue hills of Alsace, all the way across poor, devastated France. The rays of the dying sun fell upon the handle-bar of *Uncle Sam*, which the rider held in the steady, fraternal handshake that they knew so well. Back from the coast they sped, those two, along the winding road which lay on hill and in valley, bathed in the mellow glow of the first twilight. Swiftly and silently they sped. Hills rose and fell, the fair panorama of the lowlands with its quaint old houses here and there opened before them. And so they journeyed on into the din and fire and stenching suffocation and red-running streams of Picardy and Flanders—for service as required.

END

Other books by this author

Tom Slade at Black Lake

Tom Slade's Double Dare

Tom Slade with the Boys Over There

Tom Slade with the Colors

Tom Slade on Mystery Trail

Tom Slade At Temple Camp

Pee-Wee Harris on the Trail

Pee-Wee Harris Adrift

Roy Blakeley's Adventures in Camp

Roy Blakeley

Percy Keese Fitzhugh

Choose from Thousands of 1stWorldLibrary Classics By

A. M. Barnard	Booth Tarkington	Edward Everett Hale
Ada Leverson	Boyd Cable	Edward J. O'Biren
Adolphus William Ward	Bram Stoker	Edward S. Ellis
Aesop	C. Collodi	Edwin L. Arnold
Agatha Christie	C. E. Orr	Eleanor Atkins
Alexander Aaronsohn	C. M. Ingleby	Eleanor Hallowell Abbott
Alexander Kielland	Carolyn Wells	Eliot Gregory
Alexandre Dumas	Catherine Parr Traill	Elizabeth Gaskell
Alfred Gatty	Charles A. Eastman	Elizabeth McCracken
Alfred Ollivant	Charles Amory Beach	Elizabeth Von Arnim
Alice Duer Miller	Charles Dickens	Ellem Key
Alice Turner Curtis	Charles Dudley Warner	Emerson Hough
Alice Dunbar	Charles Farrar Browne	Emilie F. Carlen
Allen Chapman	Charles Ives	Emily Bronte
Alleyne Ireland	Charles Kingsley	Emily Dickinson
Ambrose Bierce	Charles Klein	Enid Bagnold
Amelia E. Barr	Charles Hanson Towne	Enilor Macartney Lane
Amory H. Bradford	Charles Lathrop Pack	Erasmus W. Jones
Andrew Lang	Charles Romyn Dake	Ernie Howard Pie
Andrew McFarland Davis	Charles Whibley	Ethel May Dell
Andy Adams	Charles Willing Beale	Ethel Turner
Angela Brazil	Charlotte M. Braeme	Ethel Watts Mumford
Anna Alice Chapin	Charlotte M. Yonge	Eugene Sue
Anna Sewell	Charlotte Perkins Stetson	Eugenie Foa
Annie Besant	Clair W. Hayes	Eugene Wood
Annie Hamilton Donnell	Clarence Day Jr.	Eustace Hale Ball
Annie Payson Call	Clarence E. Mulford	Evelyn Everett-green
Annie Roe Carr	Clemence Housman	Everard Cotes
Annonaymous	Confucius	F. H. Cheley
Anton Chekhov	Coningsby Dawson	F. J. Cross
Archibald Lee Fletcher	Cornelis DeWitt Wilcox	F. Marion Crawford
Arnold Bennett	Cyril Burleigh	Fannie E. Newberry
Arthur C. Benson	D. H. Lawrence	Federick Austin Ogg
Arthur Conan Doyle	Daniel Defoe	Ferdinand Ossendowski
Arthur M. Winfield	David Garnett	Fergus Hume
Arthur Ransome	Dinah Craik	Florence A. Kilpatrick
Arthur Schnitzler	Don Carlos Janes	Fremont B. Deering
Arthur Train	Donald Keyhoe	Francis Bacon
Atticus	Dorothy Kilner	Francis Darwin
B.H. Baden-Powell	Dougan Clark	Frances Hodgson Burnett
B. M. Bower	Douglas Fairbanks	Frances Parkinson Keyes
B. C. Chatterjee	E. Nesbit	Frank Gee Patchin
Baroness Emmuska Orczy	E. P. Roe	Frank Harris
Baroness Orczy	E. Phillips Oppenheim	Frank Jewett Mather
Basil King	E. S. Brooks	Frank L. Packard
Bayard Taylor	Earl Barnes	Frank V. Webster
Ben Macomber	Edgar Rice Burroughs	Frederic Stewart Isham
Bertha Muzzy Bower	Edith Van Dyne	Frederick Trevor Hill
Bjornstjerne Bjornson	Edith Wharton	Frederick Winslow Taylor

Friedrich Kerst
Friedrich Nietzsche
Fyodor Dostoyevsky
G.A. Henty
G.K. Chesterton
Gabrielle E. Jackson
Garrett P. Serviss
Gaston Leroux
George A. Warren
George Ade
Geroge Bernard Shaw
George Cary Eggleston
George Durston
George Ebers
George Eliot
George Gissing
George MacDonald
George Meredith
George Orwell
George Sylvester Viereck
George Tucker
George W. Cable
George Wharton James
Gertrude Atherton
Gordon Casserly
Grace E. King
Grace Gallatin
Grace Greenwood
Grant Allen
Guillermo A. Sherwell
Gulielma Zollinger
Gustav Flaubert
H. A. Cody
H. B. Irving
H. C. Bailey
H. G. Wells
H. H. Munro
H. Irving Hancock
H. R. Naylor
H. Rider Haggard
H. W. C. Davis
Haldeman Julius
Hall Caine
Hamilton Wright Mabie
Hans Christian Andersen
Harold Avery
Harold McGrath
Harriet Beecher Stowe
Harry Castlemon
Harry Coghill
Harry Houidini

Hayden Carruth
Helent Hunt Jackson
Helen Nicolay
Hendrik Conscience
Hendy David Thoreau
Henri Barbusse
Henrik Ibsen
Henry Adams
Henry Ford
Henry Frost
Henry James
Henry Jones Ford
Henry Seton Merriman
Henry W Longfellow
Herbert A. Giles
Herbert Carter
Herbert N. Casson
Herman Hesse
Hildegard G. Frey
Homer
Honore De Balzac
Horace B. Day
Horace Walpole
Horatio Alger Jr.
Howard Pyle
Howard R. Garis
Hugh Lofting
Hugh Walpole
Humphry Ward
Ian Maclaren
Inez Haynes Gillmore
Irving Bacheller
Isabel Cecilia Williams
Isabel Hornibrook
Israel Abrahams
Ivan Turgenev
J. G.Austin
J. Henri Fabre
J. M. Barrie
J. M. Walsh
J. Macdonald Oxley
J. R. Miller
J. S. Fletcher
J. S. Knowles
J. Storer Clouston
J. W. Duffield
Jack London
Jacob Abbott
James Allen
James Andrews
James Baldwin

James Branch Cabell
James DeMille
James Joyce
James Lane Allen
James Lane Allen
James Oliver Curwood
James Oppenheim
James Otis
James R. Driscoll
Jane Abbott
Jane Austen
Jane L. Stewart
Janet Aldridge
Jens Peter Jacobsen
Jerome K. Jerome
Jessie Graham Flower
John Buchan
John Burroughs
John Cournos
John F. Kennedy
John Gay
John Glasworthy
John Habberton
John Joy Bell
John Kendrick Bangs
John Milton
John Philip Sousa
John Taintor Foote
Jonas Lauritz Idemil Lie
Jonathan Swift
Joseph A. Altsheler
Joseph Carey
Joseph Conrad
Joseph E. Badger Jr
Joseph Hergesheimer
Joseph Jacobs
Jules Vernes
Julian Hawthrone
Julie A Lippmann
Justin Huntly McCarthy
Kakuzo Okakura
Karle Wilson Baker
Kate Chopin
Kenneth Grahame
Kenneth McGaffey
Kate Langley Bosher
Kate Langley Bosher
Katherine Cecil Thurston
Katherine Stokes
L. A. Abbot
L. T. Meade

L. Frank Baum
Latta Griswold
Laura Dent Crane
Laura Lee Hope
Laurence Housman
Lawrence Beasley
Leo Tolstoy
Leonid Andreyev
Lewis Carroll
Lewis Sperry Chafer
Lilian Bell
Lloyd Osbourne
Louis Hughes
Louis Joseph Vance
Louis Tracy
Louisa May Alcott
Lucy Fitch Perkins
Lucy Maud Montgomery
Luther Benson
Lydia Miller Middleton
Lyndon Orr
M. Corvus
M. H. Adams
Margaret E. Sangster
Margret Howth
Margaret Vandercook
Margaret W. Hungerford
Margret Penrose
Maria Edgeworth
Maria Thompson Daviess
Mariano Azuela
Marion Polk Angellotti
Mark Overton
Mark Twain
Mary Austin
Mary Catherine Crowley
Mary Cole
Mary Hastings Bradley
Mary Roberts Rinehart
Mary Rowlandson
M. Wollstonecraft Shelley
Maud Lindsay
Max Beerbohm
Myra Kelly
Nathaniel Hawthrone
Nicolo Machiavelli
O. F. Walton
Oscar Wilde
Owen Johnson
P.G. Wodehouse
Paul and Mabel Thorne

Paul G. Tomlinson
Paul Severing
Percy Brebner
Percy Keese Fitzhugh
Peter B. Kyne
Plato
Quincy Allen
R. Derby Holmes
R. L. Stevenson
R. S. Ball
Rabindranath Tagore
Rahul Alvares
Ralph Bonehill
Ralph Henry Barbour
Ralph Victor
Ralph Waldo Emmerson
Rene Descartes
Ray Cummings
Rex Beach
Rex E. Beach
Richard Harding Davis
Richard Jefferies
Richard Le Gallienne
Robert Barr
Robert Frost
Robert Gordon Anderson
Robert L. Drake
Robert Lansing
Robert Lynd
Robert Michael Ballantyne
Robert W. Chambers
Rosa Nouchette Carey
Rudyard Kipling
Saint Augustine
Samuel B. Allison
Samuel Hopkins Adams
Sarah Bernhardt
Sarah C. Hallowell
Selma Lagerlof
Sherwood Anderson
Sigmund Freud
Standish O'Grady
Stanley Weyman
Stella Benson
Stella M. Francis
Stephen Crane
Stewart Edward White
Stijn Streuvels
Swami Abhedananda
Swami Parmananda
T. S. Ackland

T. S. Arthur
The Princess Der Ling
Thomas A. Janvier
Thomas A Kempis
Thomas Anderton
Thomas Bailey Aldrich
Thomas Bulfinch
Thomas De Quincey
Thomas Dixon
Thomas H. Huxley
Thomas Hardy
Thomas More
Thornton W. Burgess
U. S. Grant
Upton Sinclair
Valentine Williams
Various Authors
Vaughan Kester
Victor Appleton
Victor G. Durham
Victoria Cross
Virginia Woolf
Wadsworth Camp
Walter Camp
Walter Scott
Washington Irving
Wilbur Lawton
Wilkie Collins
Willa Cather
Willard F. Baker
William Dean Howells
William le Queux
W. Makepeace Thackeray
William W. Walter
William Shakespeare
Winston Churchill
Yei Theodora Ozaki
Yogi Ramacharaka
Young E. Allison
Zane Grey